T0116223

MORALITY

BERNARD WILLIAMS

MORALITY

AN INTRODUCTION
TO ETHICS

CAMBRIDGE
UNIVERSITY PRESS

CAMBRIDGE
UNIVERSITY PRESS

Shaftesbury Road, Cambridge CB2 8EA, United Kingdom

One Liberty Plaza, 20th Floor, New York, NY 10006, USA

477 Williamstown Road, Port Melbourne, VIC 3207, Australia

314–321, 3rd Floor, Plot 3, Splendor Forum, Jasola District Centre, New Delhi – 110025, India

103 Penang Road, #05–06/07, Visioncrest Commercial, Singapore 238467

Cambridge University Press is part of Cambridge University Press & Assessment, a department of the University of Cambridge.

We share the University's mission to contribute to society through the pursuit of education, learning and research at the highest international levels of excellence.

www.cambridge.org
Information on this title: www.cambridge.org/9781107604766

First published in the USA by Harper & Row 1972
Published in Pelican Books 1973
Reissued by the Cambridge University Press 1976
Reprinted 1978, 1980, 1982, 1987, 1990
Canto edition 1993
21st printing 2021

A catalogue record for this publication is available from the British Library

ISBN   978-1-107-60476-6   Paperback

To
My Mother and Father

CONTENTS

PREFACE TO THE CANTO EDITION

THIS text was originally intended to be part of a larger book, which was to consist of several novella-length pieces by different writers, forming collectively a substantial introduction to philosophy. When the editor, Arthur Danto, invited me to write the section on moral philosophy, he made it clear that while we were encouraged to write in an introductory way, we were not being asked to write merely a survey, but rather to pursue the interests and questions that each found most interesting or fruitful. The publishers in the end decided not to put out the big book (which, granted who they were, some of us had inevitably called 'Harper's Bazaar'), and published each section separately.

At least one of those books (Richard Wollheim's *Art and Its Objects*) has grown in later life, acquiring new sections in further editions. This one, on the other hand, remains as it was. The main reason for this is that I have subsequently written other books and papers on some of the same subjects, and could see no point in loading this text with intrusive (and probably misleading) references to that later work. In the case of one topic, utilitarianism, this would have been particularly inappropriate, since in what I wrote later I tried to take account of what I had written here, and to develop rather different points; the relevant chapter here perhaps summarizes the central problem, as I see it, of the utilitarian project more compactly than I have done elsewhere.

For rather similar reasons, I have not tried to provide an up-to-date bibliography. Recent literature on subjectivism, for instance, has obviously changed and extended the questions beyond my treatment of the subject here, but to explain this so as to introduce that literature would have involved substantial further philosophical discussion. In fact, there is no bibliography, even an out-of-date one, but only a handful of references, perhaps rather idiosyncratic, to some writing that I had found helpful.

In one respect at least the book may seem dated, to the extent that it starts by complaining of a situation which no longer exists, one in which moral philosophy addressed itself to meta-ethical questions about the nature of moral judgement, the possibility of moral knowledge, and so forth, at the expense of discussing first-order ethical questions. Moral philosophy still, appropriately, discusses meta-ethical questions, but it is certainly not true any longer that first-order questions are not mentioned. On the contrary, issues such as abortion, feminism, and famine are now standardly discussed in moral philosophy courses and textbooks. I must confess that some of these discussions, assuming as they do that ethical thought is made more rational by deploying ethical theory, seem to me as distanced from real experience as the forms of uncommitted moral philosophy about which I complain here. The spirit in question is, unnervingly, the same. But the complaint is certainly different.*

There are points at which the two complaints unite. I have criticized in some more recent work the assumption often made, not just by moral philosophy but by ethical reflection more generally, that we are clear enough about what count as 'moral' considerations and sentiments, and that what moral philosophy must seek is the basis and status of these considerations, taken more or less as a whole. I have wanted to ask a prior question, about what the distinction between the 'moral' and the 'non-moral' is supposed to do for us; and I have suggested that considerations of the moral kind make sense only if they are related to other reasons for action that human beings use, and generally to their desires, needs and projects.

Those concerns are perhaps not altogether explicit in this book, and in particular it does not observe a certain verbal distinction which I have more recently found useful, between a broader conception of 'the ethical', and the narrower concerns (focused particularly on ideas of obligation) of what may be called the system of 'morality'. Others may not find this terminology helpful, but since I have suggested it, it is perhaps worth mentioning, in particular, that the title and sub-title of this book do not use those words in that way. It would surely be possible to discuss morality – in my current, restrictive sense – as an introduction to ethics (though I doubt that it would be the best way to get introduced to it); but this is not in fact what this book does. Rather, it discusses, a lot of the time, ethics

---

* I have pressed the later complaint, against the supposed power of ethical theory, in *Ethics and the Limits of Philosophy* (London: Collins, and Harvard University Press, 1985), where I also discuss some peculiarities of the 'morality system', which I mention below.

as an introduction to the problems and limitations of morality.

The placing of morality in relation to other ethical considerations and to the rest of life – in relation to happiness, for instance – is in fact a theme here, although it is not expressed in those terms. Because it does contain that theme, the book has a characteristic which I did not consciously have in mind when I wrote it, but which was pointed out to me by a classicist who had used it in his teaching, that the concerns from which it sets out are those more typical of the ancient world and its philosophies than of modernity. In a recent book,* I have tried to develop more reflectively and on a larger scale this interest in ethical ideas of the ancient world (and not only of its philosophies), and a sense of their relevance to our present situation.

Near the beginning of this book, I talk about the problems of finding a style for moral philosophy. I still think that these problems are real, and also that moral philosophy involves such problems to a greater extent than most other areas of philosophy. What I should not want to accept now is an implication to be heard in this discussion, that there might be one general solution to this problem, and that once one had found it one would know how to write moral philosophy. That cannot be so: the problems of finding a convincing, adult, and unmechanical way of approaching the subject must be faced on each occasion. Sometimes literature or history can be called upon, to give some idea of the weight or substance of ethical concepts that we use or have been used by others; analytic argument, the philos-

———
* *Shame and Necessity* (California University Press, 1993).

xiv

opher's speciality, can certainly play a part in sharpening perception. But the aim *is* to sharpen perception, to make one more acutely and honestly aware of what one is saying, thinking and feeling. Philosophy invites us (perhaps more insistently now than when this book was written) to ask whether what we say in morality is true. One thing I felt in writing this book, and feel even more now, is that it is vital not to forget another question that is to be asked both about morality and about moral philosophy, how far what we say *rings* true.

BERNARD WILLIAMS
Berkeley, March 1993.

PREFACE

WRITING about moral philosophy should be a hazard-
ous business, not just for the reasons attendant on writing about any difficult subject, or writing about
anything, but for two special reasons. The first is that
one is likely to reveal the limitations and inadequacies
of one's own perceptions more directly than in, at least,
other parts of philosophy. The second is that one could
run the risk, if one were taken seriously, of misleading
people about matters of importance. While few writers
on the subject have avoided the first hazard, very many
have avoided the second, either by making it impossible to take them seriously, or by refusing to write
about anything of importance, or both.

This sad truth is often brought forward as a particular charge against contemporary moral philosophy of
the 'analytical' or 'linguistic' style: that it is peculiarly empty and boring. In one way, as a particular
charge, this is unfair: most moral philosophy at most
times has been empty and boring, and the number of
great books in the subject (as opposed to books involved
in one way or another in morality) can be literally
counted on the fingers of one hand. The emptiness of
past works, however, has often been the emptiness of
conventional moralizing, the banal treatment of moral
issues. Contemporary moral philosophy has found an
original way of being boring, which is by not discussing
moral issues at all. Or, rather, it is not so much that a

style of moral philosophy has been evolved which cuts the connection with moral issues altogether – that, if it were possible, would have the interest of being remarkable; but the desire to reduce revealed moral commitment to a minimum and to use moral arguments in the role of being uncontentiously illustrative leaves an impression that all the important issues are off the page, somewhere, and that great caution and little imagination have been used in letting tiny corners of them appear.

There are many reasons for this situation. A central one is that contemporary views about morality itself leave an unclarity about what qualities of mind or character are particularly called upon in constructive moral thought (indeed, in some accounts of morality it is not even clear that there can be such a thing as constructive moral thought); they hence leave one all the more uneasy about whether those qualities are likely to be the qualities of philosophers, when philosophy is largely a professional and academic activity calling principally, though not exclusively, on discursive and analytical abilities. If there were such an activity as deducing substantial moral conclusions from *a priori* premises, trained philosophers might reasonably be expected to be rather specially good at it; but there is not, and the fact that if there were, then professional philosophers would stand a specially good chance of being informed about morality, is itself one of the good reasons for thinking that there could not be such an activity.

Certainly the trouble is not, as some pretend, that if the philosopher is not patently detached and even methodological, then he must be *preaching*; that cannot possibly be the only alternative. It is rather a stylistic problem, in the deepest sense of 'style' in which to discover the right style is to discover what you are really trying to do. How does one combine argument (which is after all likely to constitute the philosopher's special claim on anyone's attention) with either the longer leaps or the more concrete detail which provide the more interesting stuff of moral thought? Can the reality of complex moral situations be represented by means other than those of imaginative literature? If not, can more schematic approaches represent enough of the reality? How much of what genuinely worries anyone is responsive to general theory?

If I knew answers to these questions, I should not have to ask them now.

This essay takes a rather tortuous course, and while I have tried to signpost the major bends, it may be worth sketching a plan in advance. I start with a figure who has often been of interest, indeed a cause of concern, to moralists, as providing a challenge to morality and a demand for its justification: the amoralist, who is supposedly immune to moral considerations. Some of the most interesting questions about him, which I have barely touched on, lie not so much in what might be said to him, as in what might be said about him – what the amoralist can consistently be like. From him, we move to those who do not reject morality, but do take certain special, and it may be almost as disquieting, views about its nature: subjectivists of various kinds, and an unashamedly crass (but common) kind of relativist. Here I try to examine carefully a project very close to the heart of much modern moral philosophy, which I have called that of *defusing* subjectivism.

From there, to some considerations about goodness; and, trying to get clear about some ways a man can be good *at* certain things, and still more about things he can be good *as*, I seek to disentangle some purely logical considerations from what seem to me more substantial issues about what men are and the connection of that with goodness. Two questions in particular emerge from the many that crowd round that area: the relations of intellectual achievement to the standards of morality, and the question whether, if God existed, that would make any difference to the situation of morality. This raises some important general questions about moral and other motives. These in turn lead to some issues about the point or substance of morality, and whether it is ultimately all about human welfare or (more narrowly, perhaps) happiness. Lastly, the most simple-minded way of aiming morality at happiness, that of utilitarianism, is touched on, but only long enough to suggest how special and peculiar a system, properly understood, it is; and to point in the direction where its peculiarities are to be found. To follow them out is a task for another occasion.*

One of the many ways in which this essay is not a textbook, even an introductory and outline textbook, of moral philosophy is that it offers no systematic theory. I am unashamed about that, since it seems to me that this subject has received more over-general and over-simplified systematization, while inviting it less, than virtually any other part of philosophy. I do not mean by that that one should approach moral philosophy without preconceptions (which would be impos-

*See *A Critique of Utilitarianism*, which appears in *Utilitarianism: For and Against* (Cambridge University Press, 1973).

sible), or even without theoretical preconceptions (which might well prove static and sterile). It is merely that one's initial responsibilities should be to moral phenomena, as grasped in one's own experience and imagination, and, at the more theoretical level, to the demands of *other* parts of philosophy – in particular, of the philosophy of mind. There is no reason why moral philosophy, or again something in some respects broader, in some respects narrower, called 'value theory', should yield any interesting self-contained theory at all.

Another way in which this is not a textbook is that it leaves out large tracts of the subject. That is, at least, fully obvious. But it may help to put what is here in some better perspective if I mention one or two subjects which a larger treatment of moral philosophy should in my view have near its centre: what practical thought, and acting for a reason, are; what consistency in action is, and in moral thought; relatedly, how moral conflict is a basic fact of morality; how the notion of a *rule* is important for some, but not all, parts of morality (the present essay has nothing to say about its importance); how shaky and problematical is the distinction between the 'moral' and the 'non-moral' – above all in its most important employment, to distinguish between different sorts of human excellence.

That this essay should leave out most things of importance was inevitable; that it should follow a tortuous path, was not. Whether it was inevitable that it should fail to find an answer to the problem of how to write about moral philosophy, I do not know.

MORALITY
AN INTRODUCTION TO ETHICS

THE AMORALIST

'WHY should I do anything?' Two of the many ways of taking that question are these: as an expression of despair or hopelessness, when it means something like 'Give me a reason for doing anything; everything is meaningless'; and as sounding a more defiant note, against morality, when it means something like 'Why is there anything that I *should, ought to,* do?'

Even though we can paraphrase the question in the first spirit as 'Give me a reason ...', it is very unclear that we can in fact give the man who asks it a reason – that, starting from so far down, we could *argue* him into caring about something. We might indeed 'give him a reason' in the sense of finding something that he is prepared to care about, but that is not inducing him to care by reasoning, and it is very doubtful whether there could be any such thing. What he needs is help, or hope, not reasonings. Of course it is true that if he stays alive he will be doing *something*, rather than something else, and thus in some absolutely minimal sense he has some sort of reason, some minimal preference, for doing those things rather than other things. But to point this out gets us hardly anywhere; he does those things just mechanically, perhaps, to keep going, and they mean nothing to him. Again, if he sees his state as a reason for suicide, then that would be to make a real decision; as a way out of making any decisions, suicide comes inevitably one decision too late (as Camus points out in

Le Mythe de Sisyphe). But it would be no victory for us
or for him if it turned out there was after all just one
decision that he was prepared to acknowledge, that
one.

I do not see how it could be regarded as a defeat for
reason or rationality that it had no power against this
man's state; his state is rather a defeat for humanity.
But the man who asks the question in the second spirit
has been regarded by many moralists as providing a real
challenge to moral reasoning. He, after all, acknowledges
some reasons for doing things; he is, moreover, like
most of us some of the time. If morality can be got off
the ground rationally, then we ought to be able to get it
off the ground in an argument against him; while, in his
pure form – in which we can call him the *amoralist* –
he may not be actually persuaded, it might seem a comfort to morality if there were reasons which, if he were
rational, would persuade him.

We might ask first what motivations he does have.
He is indifferent to moral considerations, but there are
things that he cares about, and he has some real pre-
ferences and aims. They might be, presumably, pleasure
or power; or they might be something much odder, such
as some passion for collecting things. Now these ends
in themselves do not exclude some acknowledgement of
morality; what do we have to leave out to represent him
as paying no such acknowledgement? Presumably such
things as his caring about other people's interests, having any inclination to tell the truth or keep promises if
it does not suit him to do so, being disposed to reject
courses of action on the ground that they are unfair or
dishonourable or selfish. These are some of the substantial materials of morality. We should perhaps also leave

out a more formal aspect of morality, namely any disposition on his part to stand back and have the thought
that if it is 'all right' for him to act in these ways, it
must be 'all right' for others to act similarly against
him. For if he is prepared to take this stance, we might
be able to take a step towards saying that he was not a
man without a morality, but a man with a peculiar
one.

However, we need a distinction here. In one way, it
is possible for a man to think it 'all right' for everyone
to behave self-interestedly, without his having got into
any distinctively moral territory of thought at all: if,
roughly, 'it's all right' means 'I am not going to
moralize about it'. He will be in some moral territory if
'all right' means something like 'permitted', for that
would carry implications such as 'people ought not to
interfere with other people's pursuit of their own interests', and that is not a thought which, as an amoralist,
he can have. Similarly, if he objects (as he no doubt
will) to other people treating him as he treats them, this
will be perfectly consistent so long as his objecting consists just in such things as his not liking it and fighting
back. What he cannot consistently do is *resent* it or
disapprove of it, for these are attitudes within the moral
system. It may be difficult to discover whether he has
given this hostage to moral argument or not, since he
will no doubt have discovered that insincere expressions
of resentment and moral hurt serve to discourage some
of the more squeamish in his environment from hostile
action.

This illustrates, as do many of his activities, the
obvious fact that this man is a parasite on the moral
system, and he and his satisfactions could not exist as

5

they do unless others operated differently. For, in general, there can be no society without some moral rules, and he needs society; also he takes more particular advantage of moral institutions like promising and of moral dispositions of people around him. He cannot deny, as a fact, his parasitic position; but he is very resistant to suggestions of its relevance. For if we try saying 'How would it be for you if everyone behaved like that?' he will reply, 'Well, if they did, not good, I suppose – though in fact I might do better in the resulting chaos than some of the others. But the fact is, most of them are not going to do so; and if they do ever get round to it, I shall be dead by then.' The appeal to the consequences of an *imagined* universalization is an essentially moral argument, and he is, consistently, not impressed by it.

In maintaining this stance, there are several things he must, in consistency, avoid. One – as we noticed before, in effect – is any tendency to say that the more or less moral majority have *no right* to dislike him, reject him, or treat him as an enemy, if indeed they are inclined to do so (his power, or charm, or dishonesty may be such that they do not). No thoughts about justification, at least of that sort, are appropriate to him. Again, he must resist, if consistent, a more insidious tendency to think of himself as being in character really rather splendid – in particular, as being by comparison with the craven multitude notably courageous. For in entertaining such thoughts, he will run a constant danger of getting outside the world of his own desires and tastes into the region in which certain dispositions are regarded as excellent for human beings to have, or good to have in society, or such things; and while such thoughts need not lead directly to moral considerations, they give a substantial footing to them, since they immediately invite questions about what is so good about those dispositions, and it will be difficult for him to pursue those questions very far without thinking in terms of the *general* interests and needs of his fellow human beings, which would land him once more back in the world of moral thought from which he is excluding himself.

The temptation to think of himself as courageous is a particularly dangerous one, since it is itself very nearly a moral notion and draws with it a whole chain of distinctively moral reflections. This man's application of the notion will also have a presupposition which is false: namely, that the more moral citizens would be amoral if they could get away with it, or if they were not too frightened, or if they were not passively conditioned by society – if, in general, they did not suffer from inhibitions. It is the idea that they are afraid that gives him the idea of his own courage. But these presuppositions are absurd. If he means that if as an individual one could be sure of getting away with it, one would break any moral rule (the idea behind the model of Gyges' ring of invisibility in Plato's *Republic*), it is just false of many agents, and there is reason why: the more basic moral rules and conceptions are strongly internalized in upbringing, at a level from which they do not merely evaporate with the departure of policemen or censorious neighbours. This is part of what it is for them to be moral rules, as opposed to *merely* legal requirements or matters of social convention. The effects of moral education can actually be to make people *want* to act, quite often, in a non-self-interested way, and it often succeeds in making it at least quite difficult, for internal reasons, to behave appallingly.

But this, he will say, is just social conditioning; remove that, and you will find no moral motivations. – We can reject the rhetoric of the word 'conditioning'; even if there were a true theory, which there is not, which could explain all moral and similar education in terms of behaviourist learning theory, it would itself have to explain the very evident differences between successful and intelligent upbringing, which produces insight, and the production of conditioned reflexes. Then let us say instead that all moral motivation is the product of social influences, teaching, culture, etc. It is no doubt true. But virtually everything else about a man is such a product, including his language, his methods of thought, his tastes, and even his emotions, including most of the dispositions that the amoralist sets store by. – But, he may say, suppose we grant that anything complex, even my desires, are influenced by culture and environment, and in many cases produced by these; nevertheless there are *basic* impulses, of a self-interested kind, which are at the bottom of it all: these constitute what men are *really* like.

If 'basic' means 'genetically primitive', he may possibly be right: it is a matter of psychological theory. But even if true in this sense, it is once more irrelevant (to his argument, not to questions about how to bring up children); if there is such a thing as what men are *really* like, it is not identical with what very small children are like, since very small children have no language, again, nor many other things which men really have. If the test of what men are *really* like is made, rather, of how men may behave in conditions of great

8

stress, deprivation, or scarcity (the test that Hobbes, in his picture of the state of nature, imposed), one can only ask again, why should that be the test? Apart from the unclarity of its outcome, why is the test even appropriate? Conditions of great stress and deprivation are not the conditions for observing the typical behaviour of any animal nor for observing other characteristics of human beings. If someone says that if you want to see what men are *really* like, see them after they have been three weeks in a lifeboat, it is unclear why that is any better a maxim with regard to their motivations than it is with regard to their physical condition.

If there is such a thing as what men are *really* like, it may be that (in these sorts of respects, at least) it is not so different from what they are *actually* like; that is, creatures in whose lives moral considerations play an important, formative, but often insecure role.

The amoralist, then, would probably be advised to avoid most forms of self-congratulatory comparison of himself with the rest of society. The rest may, of course, have some tendency to admire him, or those may who are at such a distance that he does not tread directly on their interests and affections. He should not be too encouraged by this, however, since it is probably wish-fulfilment (which does not mean that they would be like him if they could, since a wish is different from a frustrated desire). Nor will they admire him, still less like him, if he is not recognizably human. And this raises the question, whether we have left him enough to be that.

Does he care for anybody? Is there anybody whose sufferings or distress would affect him? If we say 'no' to this, it looks as though we have produced a psychopath. If he is a psychopath, the idea of arguing him into morality is surely idiotic, but the fact that it is idiotic has equally no tendency to undermine the basis of morality or of rationality. The activity of justifying morality must surely get any point it has from the existence of an alternative – there being something to justify it *against*. The amoralist seemed important because he seemed to provide an alternative; his life, after all, seemed to have its attractions. The psychopath is, in a certain way, important to moral thought; but his importance lies in the fact that he appals us, and we must seek some deeper understanding of how and why he appals us. His importance does not lie in his having an appeal as an alternative form of life.

The amoralist we loosely sketched before did seem to have possibly more appeal than this; one might picture him as having some affections, occasionally caring for what happens to somebody else. Some stereotype from a gangster movie might come to mind, of the ruthless and rather glamorous figure who cares about his mother, his child, even his mistress. He is still recognizably amoral, in the sense that no general considerations weigh with him, and he is extremely short on fairness and similar considerations. Although he acts for other people from time to time, it all depends on how he happens to feel. With this man, of course, in actual fact arguments of moral philosophy are not going to work; for one thing, he always has something he would rather do than listen to them. This is not the point (though it is more of a point than some discussions of moral argument would lead one to suppose). The point is rather that he provides a model in terms of which we may glimpse what morality needs in order to get off the ground, even though it is unlikely in practice to get off the ground in a conversation with him.

He gives us, I think, almost enough. For he has the notion of doing something *for* somebody, because that person needs something. He operates with this notion in fact only when he is so inclined; but it is not itself the notion of his being so inclined. Even if he helps these people because he wants to, or because he likes them, and for no other reason (not that, so far as these particular actions are concerned, he needs to improve on those excellent reasons), what he wants to do is *to help them in their need*, and the thought he has when he likes someone and acts in this way is 'they need help', not the thought 'I like them and they need help'. This is a vital point: this man is capable of thinking in terms of others' interests, and his failure to be a moral agent lies (partly) in the fact that he is only intermittently and capriciously disposed to do so. But there is no bottomless gulf between this state and the basic dispositions of morality. There are people who need help who are not people who at the moment he happens to want to help, or likes; and there are other people who like and want to help other particular people in need. To get him to consider their situation seems rather an extension of his imagination and his understanding, than a discontinuous step onto something quite different, the 'moral plane'. And if we could get him to consider their situation, in the sense of thinking about it and imagining it, he might conceivably start to show some consideration for it: we extend his sympathies. And if we can get him to extend his sympathies to less immediate persons who need help, we might be able to do it for less immediate persons whose interests have

11

been violated, and so get him to have some primitive grasp on notions of fairness. If we can get him all this way, then, while he has no doubt an extremely shaky hold on moral considerations, he has some hold on them; at any rate, he is not the amoralist we started with.

This model is not meant to sketch the outline of a construction of the whole of morality from the possibility of sympathy and the extensions of sympathy: that would be impossible. (Even Hume, who perhaps came nearest to it, did not attempt that. His system, among the many interesting and valuable things that it contains, has a distinction between the 'natural' and the 'artificial' virtues which is relevant to this point.) The model is meant to suggest just one thing: that if we grant a man with even a minimal concern for others, then we do not have to ascribe to him any fundamentally new kind of thought or experience to include him in the world of morality, but only what is recognizably an extension of what he already has. He is not very far into it, and it is an extensive territory: as we saw in drawing up the amoralist, you have to travel quite a long way to get out of it. But the man with the extended sympathies, the ability to think about the needs of people beyond his own immediate involvement, is recognizably in it.

It does not follow from this that having sympathetic concern for others is a necessary condition of being in the world of morality, that the way sketched is the *only* way 'into morality'. It does not follow from what has so far been said; but it is true.

Some of the considerations touched on here, about moral and other motivations, we shall come back to later. I shall now turn to someone who is also found upsetting by morality, but in a different way from the amoralist. This man is content that he should have a morality, but points out that other people have different ones – and insists that there is no way of choosing between them. He is the subjectivist.

SUBJECTIVISM: FIRST THOUGHTS

CONSIDER three statements, each of which, in its different way, expresses a view that moral opinions, or moral judgements, or moral outlooks are 'merely subjective':

(a) A man's moral judgements merely state (or express) his own attitudes.

(b) Moral judgements can't be proved, established, shown to be true as scientific statements can; they are matters of individual opinion.

(c) There are no moral facts; there are only the sorts of facts that science or common observation can discover, and the values that men place on those facts.

The three statements come very close to one another, and in discussions of subjectivism and objectivism one often finds versions of the three being used virtually interchangeably. They are, indeed, genuinely related to one another. Yet they are significantly different. The first, (a), expresses what might be called in a broad sense a *logical* or linguistic view: it purports to tell us something about what moral remarks are or do. The second, (b), introduces a set of notions not present in the first, notions connected with the concept of *knowledge*, and may be taken to express an *epistemological* view about moral judgements. The third statement, (c), is the vaguest and least tangible of the three, and shows on its surface the danger of collapsing, partly or completely, into one or other of the first two: which is what many philosophers would claim it must do. Yet in its

14

inadequate way it seems to gesture towards something which is closest of all to what has concerned many who have been worried about moral objectivity: the idea that there is no moral order 'out there' – out there, in the world, are only the sorts of things and the sorts of facts that science, and the more everyday processes of human enquiry of which science is a refinement, deal. *Alles anderes ist Menschenwerk.* Statement (c) can be said – using the word in an unambitious way – to express a *metaphysical* view.

The metaphysical view brings out most explicitly something that is latent in all the three statements, a distinction between fact and value. A central concern of much modern moral philosophy has been the distinction between fact and value. One important form that this concern has taken has been to emphasize the distinction, while rejecting the supposedly disquieting consequences of it, by trying to show either that they are not consequences, or that they are not disquieting. This project of *defusing* subjectivism (as it might be called) can be expressed in terms of our three subjectivist statements roughly as follows: that, in so far as they are defensible, they come to the same thing; and that what they come to is both not alarming and essential to the nature of morality (the point that is essential to the nature of morality seems sometimes to be thought, oddly, to imply just by itself the point that it is not alarming).

This project we shall follow, with interruptions, for some while. It starts as follows. Statement (a), first of all, is either false or harmless. It is false if it claims that moral judgements *state* their utterer's attitudes. For if this were so, they would be simply autobiographical

remarks, replaceable without loss by statements explicitly of the form 'My attitude towards this . . .' or 'I
feel . . .' But if this were so, there would be no inter-
personal moral disagreements; two persons expressing
what we would normally take to be conflicting views
would not be expressing conflicting views at all, but
would be, rather, like two persons on a boat, one of
whom says that he feels sick while the other says that
he, on the other hand, does not. But it is an evident fact
that there are genuine moral disagreements, and
that moral views can conflict. Moral judgements must
(at least to this extent) mean what we take them to
mean; and what we take them to mean, the way we use
them, is such that they do not merely make autobiographical claims, but a sort of claim which is being
rejected by someone who utters a contrary moral judgement. Thus they do not merely describe the speaker's
own attitude.

This argument, however, does not dispose of the possibility that moral utterances, while they do not directly
describe, may nevertheless have the function of expressing, the utterer's attitude. This claim in itself is incon-
testable and harmless; for in itself it comes to no
more than saying that a man who makes a moral judgement can (if that judgement is sincere) be said to be
expressing his attitude to a certain moral issue, and this
does not support any distinctively subjectivist view of
moral judgements: a man who sincerely makes a factual judgement may be said to be expressing his belief
about a factual issue, but that does not support a subjectivist view of factual judgements. The subjectivist
interpretation comes in when one says that one who
makes a moral judgement expresses his attitude, and

that is all there is to be said about it. In particular the subjectivist force of (a) lies in a suggestion that there is no question of the attitudes expressed in moral judgements being right or wrong, whereas there is a question of the beliefs expressed in factual judgements being true or false.

Now that the thesis has regained a distinctively subjectivist form it will be said that it is false. For – appealing once more to the ways in which moral judgements are actually made and treated – it is not true that there is no question of moral attitudes being right or wrong. One of their distinguishing marks, as against mere expressions of taste or preference, for instance in matters of food, is that we take seriously the idea of a man's being wrong in his moral views; indeed, the very concept of a moral *view* marks a difference here, leaning as it does in the direction of belief rather than of mere taste or preference. It is precisely a mark of morality that *de gustibus non disputandum* is a maxim which does not apply to it.

To this it might be replied that the fact that moral attitudes can be called 'right' or 'wrong', and that the question of their rightness or wrongness is taken seriously, does not in any ultimate sense help to transcend subjectivism. It shows not that moral attitudes are more than (merely) attitudes, but that they are attitudes which we get disturbed about; that it matters to us to secure similarity of attitude within society. The use of the language of 'right' and 'wrong' can be seen as part of the apparatus of securing agreement, marking off those who disagree and so forth; it remains the case that all we have are people's attitudes towards different sorts of conduct, personality, social institutions, etc.

Yet this account, in its turn, seems inadequate to the facts: it must at least underestimate the logical complexity of the situation. Notably it fails to account for the undoubted facts that a man may be in a state of moral doubt, which he may resolve – that a man can nonarbitrarily change his mind about a moral matter, not merely in the individual case, but on a general issue, and for reasons. Thus a man previously convinced that a permissive attitude towards abortion was wrong, might change his view on this, and not merely (for instance) because he felt lonely in a group which held the permissive attitude. No doubt many writers on moral philosophy overestimate the extent to which people are led by rational considerations to modify their moral views; those writers ignore the evident extent to which attitudes are modified by factors such as the desire to conform with one group or nonconform with another – the groups themselves not being chosen in the light of moral reasons, but rather determined by the individual's situation and needs. But this is, in one sense, beside the point. For even if moral attitudes were rarely *determined* by reasons, and the reasons advanced in their support were rationalizations, our model of moral attitudes and moral judgements must at least be complex enough to leave a place for the rationalizations. It is only if the position to which a man is led by these forces satisfies some conditions of being the sort of position to which reasons are relevant that we can understand it as a moral position at all.

However, even if moral attitudes are of a character to admit of support and attack by reasons, and the deployment of reasons in reaching a conclusion; nevertheless it may be said that these activities are possible only within a framework of given assumptions. If people can argue one with another about an individual moral issue or a question of principle, this is only because there are moral attitudes in the background which are not in dispute and in the light of which the argument goes on. Putting this point in a rather stronger form, it might be said that it is only about the *application* of accepted moral views that the argument goes on. So where there is no background of moral agreement, there can be no argument. At this point the subjectivist attitude can reappear, claiming now that all that has been shown by the considerations about exchanging reasons is that the morality of a man or a society is to some degree general and systematic and that general attitudes can be applied to less general cases. When we get outside the framework of agreed general attitudes, there is no further argument, and no way of showing any position to be right or wrong.

This comes very close to our second formulation, (b), of subjectivism; we have been led to it, it seems, by modifications of the first formulation. One might, however, want to change one element that came naturally into the formulation of (b), and, with that, one implication of the term 'subjectivism'. For when one turns to the issue of ultimate disagreements, it is natural to take as the unit which holds a set of moral attitudes, the society rather than the individual – not in order to hypostasize societies, but to draw attention to the point that there are limits to the degree of ultimate disagreement that can exist within a society (for without some degree of moral homogeneity it would not be a society); but there are no limits, at least of that kind, on disagreement beween societies.

INTERLUDE: RELATIVISM

LET us at this stage of the argument about subjectivism take a brief rest and look round a special view or assemblage of views which has been built on the site of moral disagreements between societies. This is *relativism*, the anthropologist's heresy, possibly the most absurd view to have been advanced even in moral philosophy. In its vulgar and unregenerate form (which I shall consider, since it is both the most distinctive and the most influential form) it consists of three propositions: that 'right' means (can only be coherently understood as meaning) 'right for a given society'; that 'right for a given society' is to be understood in a functionalist sense; and that (therefore) it is wrong for people in one society to condemn, interfere with, etc., the values of another society. A view with a long history, it was popular with some liberal colonialists, notably British administrators in places (such as West Africa) in which white men held no land. In that historical role, it may have had, like some other muddled doctrines, a beneficent influence, though modern African nationalism may well deplore its tribalist and conservative implications.

Whatever its results, the view is clearly inconsistent, since it makes a claim in its third proposition, about what is right and wrong in one's dealings with other societies, which uses a *nonrelative* sense of 'right' not allowed for in the first proposition. The claim that human sacrifice, for instance, was 'right for' the

Ashanti comes to be taken as saying that human sacrifice was right among the Ashanti, and this in turn as saying that human sacrifice among the Ashanti was right; i.e., we had no business to interfere with it. But this last is certainly not the sort of claim allowed by the theory. The most the theory can allow is the claim that it was right for (i.e., functionally valuable for) our society not to interfere with Ashanti society, and, first, this is certainly not all that was meant, and, second, is very dubiously true.

Apart from its logically unhappy attachment of a nonrelative morality of toleration or non-interference to a view of morality as relative, the theory suffers in its functionalist aspects from some notorious weaknesses of functionalism in general, notably difficulties that surround the identification of 'a society'. If 'society' is regarded as a cultural unit, identified in part through its values, then many of the functionalist propositions will cease to be empirical propositions and become bare tautologies: it is tediously a necessary condition of the survival of a group-with-certain-values that the group should retain those values. At the other extreme, the survival of a society could be understood as the survival of certain persons and their having descendants, in which case many functionalist propositions about the necessity of cultural survival will be false. When in Great Britain some Welsh nationalists speak of the survival of the Welsh language as a condition of the survival of Welsh society, they manage sometimes to convey an impression that it is a condition of the survival of Welsh people, as though the forgetting of Welsh were literally lethal.

In between these two extremes is the genuinely interesting territory, a province of informative social science, where there is room for such claims as that a given practice or belief is integrally connected with much more of a society's fabric than may appear on the surface, that it is not an excrescence, so that discouragement or modification of this may lead to much larger social change than might have been expected; or, again, that a certain set of values or institutions may be such that if they are lost, or seriously changed, the people in the society, while they may physically survive, will do so only in a deracinated and hopeless condition. Such propositions, if established, would of course be of first importance in deciding what to do; but they cannot take over the work of deciding what to do.

Here, and throughout the questions of conflict of values between societies, we need (and rarely get) some mildly realistic picture of what decisions might be being made by whom, of situations to which the considerations might be practically relevant. Of various paradigms that come to mind, one is that of conflict, such as the confrontation of other societies with Nazi Germany. Another is that of control, where (to eliminate further complications of the most obvious case, colonialism) one might take such a case as that of the relations of the central government of Ghana to residual elements of traditional Ashanti society. In neither case would functionalist propositions in themselves provide any answers at all. Still less will they where a major issue is whether a given group should be realistically or desirably regarded as 'a society' in a relevant sense, or whether its values and its future are to be integrally related to those of a larger group – as with the case of blacks in the United States.

22

The central confusion of relativism is to try to conjure out of the fact that societies have differing attitudes and values an *a priori* nonrelative principle to determine the attitude of one society to another; this is impossible. If we are going to say that there are ultimate moral disagreements between societies, we must include, in the matters they can disagree about, their attitudes to other moral outlooks. It is also true, however, that there are inherent features of morality that tend to make it difficult to regard a morality as applying only to a group. The element of universalization which is present in any morality, but which applies under tribal morality perhaps only to members of the tribe, progressively comes to range over persons as such. Less formally, it is essential (as was remarked earlier) to morality and its role in any society that certain sorts of reactions and motivations should be strongly internalized, and these cannot merely evaporate because one is confronted with human beings in another society. Just as *de gustibus non disputandum* is not a maxim which applies to morality, neither is 'when in Rome do as the Romans do', which is at best a principle of etiquette.

Nor is it just a case of doing as the Romans do, but of putting up with it. Here it would be a platitude to point out that of course someone who gains wider experience of the world may rightly come to regard some moral reaction of his to unfamiliar conduct as parochial and will seek to modify or discount it. There are many important distinctions to be made here between the kinds of thoughts appropriate to such a process in different cases: sometimes he may cease to regard a certain issue as a moral matter at all, sometimes he may come to see that what abroad looked the same as something he would have deplored at home was actually, in morally relevant respects, a very different thing. (Perhaps – though one can scarcely believe it – there were some missionaries or others who saw the men in a polygamous society in the light of seedy bigamists at home.) But it would be a particular moral view, and one both psychologically and morally implausible, to insist that these adaptive reactions were the only correct ones, that confronted with practices which are found and felt as inhuman, for instance, there is an *a priori* demand of acceptance. In the fascinating book by Bernal de Diaz, who went with Cortez to Mexico, there is an account of what they all felt when they came upon the sacrificial temples. This morally unpretentious collection of bravos was genuinely horrified by the Aztec practices. It would surely be absurd to regard this reaction as merely parochial or self-righteous. It rather indicated something which their conduct did not always indicate, that they regarded the Indians as men rather than as wild animals.

It is fair to press this sort of case, and in general the cases of actual confrontation. 'Every society has its own standards' may be, even if confused, a sometimes useful maxim of social study; as a maxim of social study it is also painless. But what, after all, is one supposed to do if confronted with a human sacrifice? – not a real question for many of us, perhaps, but a real question for Cortez. 'It wasn't their business,' it may be said; 'they had no right to be there anyway.' Perhaps – though this, once more, is necessarily a nonrelative moral judgement itself. But even if they had no right to be there, it is a matter for real moral argument what would *follow* from that. For if a burglar comes across

24

the owner of the house trying to murder somebody, is he morally obliged not to interfere because he is trespassing?

None of this is to deny the obvious facts that many have interfered with other societies when they should not have done; have interfered without understanding; and have interfered often with a brutality greater than that of anything they were trying to stop. I am saying only that it cannot be a consequence of the nature of morality itself that no society ought ever to interfere with another, or that individuals from one society confronted with the practices of another ought, if rational, to react with acceptance. To draw these consequences is the characteristic (and inconsistent) step of vulgar relativism.

SUBJECTIVISM: FURTHER THOUGHTS

THE enticements of vulgar relativism are not very tempting. But its central error is quite important; and that it is an error has a significance beyond that particular doctrine, concerned as that is with the relations between societies. It is possible for someone persuaded of subjectivist views to cease to care about moral issues. (This is different from ceasing to regard something as, in itself, a moral issue. Thus it is both possible and reasonable to suppose that there is no distinctively sexual morality, in the sense of moral considerations that govern sexual relationships and nothing else; while admitting the extremely obvious fact that sexual relationships are profoundly and specially liable to give rise to moral issues, of trust, exploitation, unconcern for the interests of third parties and so forth.) A man confronted with some monstrous political injustice, for instance, may feel no confidence in protesting or fighting against it because, as he says, 'Who's to judge?,' or 'It's only my feelings against theirs,' or something like that.

In so far as there is any traceable intellectual link between the subjectivism and the indifference, it must involve something like the relativist error. For the thought must be something like this: 'Because subjectivism is true, I am not justified in protesting.' If this is right, it must be so either because, if subjectivism is true, no one is justified in doing anything; or because, if subjectivism is true, he is specially not justified in protesting. If the first of these, then the inflicters of the injustice are not justified in what they are doing either, nor is this man justified in *not* protesting, and these considerations remove any *basis* he was supposed to have for his indifference. In any case, the argument in this version has surely gone too far, even for subjectivism; since subjectivism did not claim it to be impossible to think that anything was justified, but only that when a given man thinks something is justified, he cannot in the end be proved wrong. The man we are arguing with has somehow got from that to a position in which no one (however subjectively) can think something justified, and that must be a mistake; unless, of course, subjectivism is inconsistent, in which case subjectivism is false, and the argument is over anyway.

Let us try the second alternative, then, that because subjectivism is true, he is specially not justified in protesting. Why should this be so? 'Well', he may say, 'they think they are right, and who am I to say that they are wrong?' But the apparent force of this is entirely gained from its subtly moving out of the subjectivist arena and importing the idea that there is such a thing as objective rightness, only he is not sure whether these other people's actions possess it or not. Sticking to the subjectivist path, he must recognize that if he chooses to think that they are wrong and that he is right in protesting, then no one can say he is wrong either, and he can be no less justified in protesting than they are in doing what they are doing. Another way of putting this point is this: 'perhaps they are right' must be one of *his* moral thoughts. If he also has the thought 'They are wrong (only I am not justified in protesting)', he has inconsistent moral thoughts within his own system, and subjectivism never required him to do that. In fact, of course, the thought 'Who am I to say that they are wrong?' is one that is had, not within his own subjective compound, but in mid-air above his own and the other people's; it tries to stand outside all moral positions (including the thinker's own) and yet still be a moral thought. But this mid-air place, by subjectivism itself, is not a place in which anyone can have a moral thought.

These sorts of reasons show why the defusers of subjectivism say that it leaves everything where it was and cannot possibly logically imply indifferentism or any other practical attitude. (They move perhaps rather rapidly from that to the claim that their views cannot *encourage* any such attitudes, perhaps on the questionable ground that I cannot be responsible for muddles that people get into as a result of what I say.) But does subjectivism leave everything where it was? Surely not *everything*. The dialectical skeins we just went through are, I think, perfectly valid, as showing that indifferentism could not follow from subjectivism. But the reason why this is so is that the argument for indifferentism requires, and subjectivism forbids, the mid-air position. But in forbidding the mid-air position, subjectivism *seems* to have taken something away, for we at least seem to recognize the mid-air position (for instance, in some of subjectivism's own statements). Another way of putting our bafflement is that we seem in these arguments to have been given no special reason why the mid-air position is debarred to *morality*. It was said that the mid-air position was no place for a moral thought. But it does seem to be a place for some sorts of thought, in particular, factual thought. Indeed, subjectivism itself (see (b) and (c) of our original formulations, given above), insists on the contrast between moral attitudes and factual beliefs, regarding the latter as 'objective' in a way that the first are not. The subjectivist leaves us, and may mean to leave us, with an uneasy feeling that factual beliefs have got, and moral beliefs lack, something that it is nice to have: that factual beliefs and science are somehow *solider* than morality.

But still, it will be said, subjectivism leaves everything where it was, so far as morality is concerned, though not perhaps so far as muddled feelings about morality are concerned. Even granted the contrast of solidity we cannot draw any practical conclusions. We cannot, in particular, conclude (as some today are obviously inclined to conclude) that since science is objective and morality is not, we are objectively justified in *devoting ourselves* to science, while only subjectively justified in protesting against injustice. For devoting oneself to science is as much a practical activity as any other, and there is no more reason why that one should be objectively justified rather than any other. Justifications for doing objective subjects are not objective justifications for doing those subjects, any more than the fact that there are deductive justifications of the theorems of *Principia Mathematica* means that there are deductive justifications of the projects of reading, rehearsing, or discovering the theorems of *Principia Mathematica*. All these are instances of that strangely tempting fallacy, the 'fat oxen' principle: who drives fat oxen must himself be fat.

Equally, though more subtly, the fact that 'pragmatic' political policies (i.e., policies which apply sophisticated technical considerations to the pursuit of self-interest) can be evaluated one against another with greater expectations of expert agreement than more idealistic policies often achieve, does not, even if true, show that we are on more objective and solid ground in adopting pragmatic rather than idealistic policies. Once we have adopted them we may be on more objective ground in working them, i.e., in deciding what to do next; but we never get on to more objective ground with reference to the question whether we ought to be doing this sort of thing at all. We are merely more comfortable, and if among the sophisticated experts, in work.

So subjectivism, even with its unsettling contrast between morality and science, is still not logically committed to producing practical consequences. It cannot even yield the conclusion that we are more solidly justified in *having* factual beliefs than moral ones; or on more objective ground in pursuing a factual question than pursuing a moral one; or objectively justified in seeking the truth about anything; or in trying to find scientific explanations of phenomena rather than resting content with superstition. For all it gave us was that factual and scientific beliefs were objective; that we should seek factual or scientific beliefs is not itself a factual or scientific belief.

Perhaps the subjectivist will readily grant these points. The unsettling contrast which he insists on between factual enquiry and moral thought is not a contrast in the grounds for starting on or pursuing those activities – rather, it is a contrast in what those two sorts of activities are, in what goes on when one is engaged in them. In particular, it is a contrast concerning

30

the nature and extent of disagreement which people engaged in those activities may, in the nature of the case, encounter. So let us look more closely at what the subjectivist has to say, in this central respect, about the unsettling contrast.

He may start by saying that if we engage in factual or scientific enquiry, then, facts being as they are, we are bound to reach some agreed scientific or factual beliefs; but we are not bound, because we engage in moral thought, and the facts are so, to reach some agreed moral beliefs. There is one element in this answer which has to be corrected straight away. For it is of course not true that if the facts are so, we are bound (granted factual thought) to reach some agreed factual beliefs: the facts may be hidden from us. The most we can say is that if we recognize that the facts are so, we are bound to reach some agreed factual beliefs. And this is a tautology, since our recognizing the facts to be so entails our reaching some agreed factual beliefs. Perhaps the subjectivist can improve on this unexciting proposition by saying something like this: that if two observers are in the same observational situation, and have the same concepts and are not defective as observers, etc., then they will reach the same factual beliefs about that situation. If the 'etc.' in this can be handled so as to make the statement true, it will almost certainly emerge as necessarily true as well. All right, says the subjectivist; but *this* is not necessarily true, indeed is not true at all: that if two observers are in the same observational situation, have the same concepts, etc., then they are bound to reach the same *moral* beliefs – and there is the contrast. But, we may say, are we sure that this latter is not true if we posit that they have the same

31

moral concepts – which is surely the fair parallel? No, it is not true even then, the subjectivist says; for if they have, as they might, rather minimal moral concepts, such as merely the concept of *what one ought to do*, they can agree on all the facts and disagree morally.

This is a central position of many philosophers who insist on the fact/value distinction. They represent different moral outlooks as all using some common, skeletal, moral concept and giving it different fillings or contents. Now we might point out that a lot of moral thought does not operate with such impoverished concepts, that we standardly think in terms of more complex ideas of virtues, types of wrong action, etc., notions of *theft*, for instance, or *cowardice*, or *loyalty*, or *the duties of one's job*. With those more substantial concepts, there is much greater hope that if we use the same concepts, we will reach agreement, or at least the sorts of disagreement which we may reasonably expect, and which are less unnerving. But the subjectivist will say that there is this asymmetry, that in scientific or factual contexts, if two observers have different concepts they may ultimately find either that the concepts are in fact equivalent, or else find reason for preferring one to the other in terms of predictive success, explanatory power, and so forth, and there is no parallel to this in the moral case.

Even if we abandon the naïve view (which some subjectivists, in working their contrast, are attached to) that science 'proves' things; even if we accept that what science does is eliminate hypotheses and that there are infinitely many hypotheses which have never been eliminated because they are too dotty for anyone to bother to test them (a point I have heard Hilary Put-

nam make); nevertheless, there are eliminatory procedures which must be respected by persons within the
scientific framework, and even the conceptual disagreements may with luck yield to impersonally accepted
criteria. Yet for some disagreements between persons
or groups both engaged in recognizably moral thought,
no such procedures exist. The contrast – some contrast
– exists.

But why should it not? This, finally, might be the
point at which a philosopher who had been arguing
with the subjectivist all this time might at last turn
round and say: of course the contrast exists; morality
is not just like science or factual knowledge, and it is
essential that it should not be. The point of morality is
not to mirror the world, but to change it; it is concerned
with such things as principles of action, choice, responsibility. The fact that men of equal intelligence, factual
knowledge, and so forth, confronted with the same
situation, may morally disagree shows something about
morality – that (roughly) you cannot pass the moral
buck on to how the world is. But that does not show (as
subjectivism originally seemed to insinuate) that there
is something *wrong* with it.

Some such statement – and I have only blocked it in
very roughly – will express the culmination of the project of what I called 'defusing' subjectivism. It has, I
think, to be granted some success. The most obvious
ways in which somebody might be unnerved by subjectivism seem to have been blocked. Thus, to revert
once again to the indifferentism we discussed before,
the 'defuser' can arrange some of the subjectivist's
materials into the following argument. We observe that
when men of equal scientific or historical competence,

equal perceptual and intellectual abilities, etc., disagree strongly about some scientific or historical matter, there is good reason for them to stop disagreeing so strongly, and recognize something which their very disagreement, granted their knowledge and skills, reveals, namely that the matter is *uncertain*: it is rational for them, and third parties, to suspend judgement. One may be tempted to think that the same should obtain in cases of moral disagreement; but this will be a mistake. It depends on first contrasting morality and factual knowledge, and then assimilating them. For the vital difference is that the disagreement in morality involves what should be done, and involves, on each side, caring about what happens; and once you see this difference, you see equally that it could not possibly be a requirement of rationality that you should stop caring about these things because someone else disagrees with you.

This, and the similar arguments, do seem to me to show that the defusing operation, in certain vital respects, has succeeded. Has it totally succeeded? If it has, then we were wrong, some time back, in feeling uneasy because subjectivism banned, for morality but not for factual beliefs, something we called the 'mid-air position'. But, I think, we were not entirely wrong, in feeling that unease – perhaps we can now see why.

If I have a factual disagreement with a man, I might think: 'I believe that p, he believes that not-p. Perhaps he is right.' The natural way of taking this is as an expression of doubt, of somewhat shaken confidence; the way I mean 'perhaps he is right' implies that while I still believe that p, I do not believe it as strongly as all that. In this way of taking it, it can be painlessly paralleled for the moral case; for if I think 'perhaps he is right,' this will naturally be taken as an expression of somewhat shaken confidence also. But now, in the factual case, there is a possible thought which seems rather similar, but is not the same: the thought 'I am convinced that p, but it is possible for all that that not-p,' where this is not an expression of *doubt* at all, but rather registers the impersonal consideration that how things are is independent of my belief; however they are, they are, whatever I believe. We do not know exactly what content to assign to this thought, but unless we have the most drastic philosophical views, we are convinced that it has a content: and the defuser will agree. But even defused subjectivism leaves no parallel thought possible on the moral side: for subjectivism, however defused, there just is no content to 'I am convinced that racial discrimination is intrinsically wrong, but it is possible for all that, that it is not,' except things like 'How convinced am I?' or 'I suppose somebody might make me change my mind.'

Such a contrast (and it, and related contrasts, need proper investigation, which we cannot attempt here) might make us agree with the third subjectivist formula we originally introduced: there are no ethical facts. Yet once more the defuser will say: this is just one more formulation of what I said already, and of something essential, not detrimental, to morality. For I have already said that moral thought is essentially practical; it is not its business to mirror the world. – But now we might reply: you said that it was not its business to mirror the world of empirical facts, and we agreed. But did we agree that it mirrored no facts at all? And here the locus of our dissatisfaction may become clearer in the thought that the reason why even defused subjectivism seems to have left something out is that moral thinking *feels* as though it mirrored something, as though it were constrained to follow, rather than be freely creative. When we see further that many defusing philosophers express the essential difference between factual and moral thought in terms of a contrast between the intellect and the *will*, and represent the responsibilities of morality in terms of our *deciding* on certain moral principles – then we have reason to be dissatisfied, either with them, or, if they are right, with moral thought. For certainly the consciousness of a principle of action as freely decided upon is very unlike the consciousness of a moral principle, which is rather of something that has to be *acknowledged*. If it is then said that there is just a psychological explanation of that – then moral thought seems a cheat, presenting itself to us as too like something which it is not.

These remarks only gesture towards a centre of dissatisfaction. They leave almost everything to be done: and not perhaps first in moral philosophy. For instance, we need to distinguish two things run together in what was just said, the idea of realism – that thought has a subject matter which is independent of the thought – and the idea of thought being constrained to certain conclusions. Thus mathematical thought has the latter property, but it is a deep and unsettled question in the philosophy of mathematics how far we should or can think in realist terms about the subject matter of mathematics.

Here I shall leave the direct discussion of subjectivism and issues that it raises, with the conclusion that defused subjectivism does not leave everything where it was, but that it does leave more where it was than we might have thought when we started. If subjectivism, however, defused, is true, things are with morality not quite as they seemed; but the fraud, we might say, justifies at most resentment rather than panic. We shall not however lose sight of the idea of constraints on moral thought, the limitations on the creation of values. We shall come round to them by another route, through the idea of goodness. To talk about goodness, we shall start with 'good'.

'GOOD'

THE use of the word 'good' has provided a focus for many discussions of basic issues in moral philosophy; while it would be a mistake to think that this word, or its approximate equivalents in other languages, could possibly bear by itself the weight of the issues, nevertheless the consideration of it provides a useful lever for lifting up some of them. We shall start with some logical considerations: these will lead us to things of greater moral substance.

As Aristotle observed, 'good' is used of many different sorts of things, of things indeed in different categories. While in one way we do not mean the same when we apply it to these different sorts of things – in this sense, that what makes a general a good general is different from what makes a doctor a good doctor – nevertheless the word is not just ambiguous: we could not tidy language up and say just what we want to say now by replacing 'good' with a different expression in each of these occurrences.

More than one theory in recent times has tried to provide a model to show that 'good' is genuinely unambiguous. One such attempt was that of G. E. Moore, who claimed that goodness was a simple indefinable property like yellowness, but that, unlike yellowness, it was *nonnatural* – that is to say (roughly), it was not the sort of property whose presence or absence could be established by empirical investigation, although (in a way left very obscure by his theory) observation of a thing's empirical characteristics was doubtless relevant to the apprehension of goodness.

Apart from its evidently mysterious and unexplanatory character, there is a logical objection to Moore's account. A very important feature of 'good' is that, in many of its occurrences, it functions as an *attributive* and not as a *predicative* adjective (as P. T. Geach has expressed the distinction).* 'Yellow', for instance, is a predicative adjective, because a sentence such as

That is a yellow bird

admits of the analysis

That is a bird and it is yellow.

By the same token, from the two sentences

That is a yellow bird
A bird is an animal

we can infer the conclusion

That is a yellow animal.

But the sentence

He is a good cricketer

cannot be analyzed as

He is a cricketer and he is good

nor can we validly infer from

He is a good cricketer
A cricketer is a man

to

He is a good man.

*P. T. Geach, 'Good and Evil', *Analysis*, Vol. 17 (1956).

An adjective which has this latter characteristic, that it is logically glued to the substantive it qualifies, may be called an attributive adjective; or, more precisely, a use in which it is so glued may be called an attributive use of it. Now Moore's account claimed that 'good' was like 'yellow' in standing for a simple quality, though unlike it in that the quality was nonnatural; and, mysterious as this is, it must at least imply that the logical behaviour of 'good' as an adjective must be like that of 'yellow'. But it is not, and so Moore's account must be rejected not just as unilluminating, but as radically misguided.

Another important attributive adjective is 'real' – an assertion that something is real can be understood only if we can answer the question 'a real what?'. This is illustrated by the situation in the art world, in which collectors are interested in acquiring the work of certain forgers, so that it can be in people's interests to forge forgeries: thus the question might arise whether this picture was a real Van Meegeren, everyone knowing that at any rate it was not a real Vermeer.

The characteristic of attributiveness needs, however, deeper exploration if we are to get an understanding of 'good'. We can see by the tests that 'large' is attributive: thus there is no valid inference from

(a) This is a large mouse
(b) A mouse is an animal

to

(c) This is a large animal.

The explanation of the failure of this inference, and of the attributiveness of 'large', is clear – it is that 'large' is a comparative term, and 'This is a large mouse' means something like 'This is a mouse larger than most mice'. By a similar analysis the conclusion (c) means something like 'This is an animal larger than most animals', and we can see why the inference fails. What can be validly inferred from these premises, on the comparative analysis, is

(d) This is an animal larger than most mice

and indeed this conclusion does follow.

Is the attributiveness of 'good' to be explained in the same way? It can hardly be that all attributiveness could be so explained – a real Van Meegeren is not one more real than most Van Meegerens. But it is more plausible to suggest that 'good' in 'good *F*' is attributive because *'good F'* means something like 'better than most *Fs*'. But further consideration shows that this will not do. We have just seen that on the comparative analysis of 'large' we can get validly from the premises (a) and (b) to the conclusion (d). If 'good' were attributive because it is comparative, then similarly we could get from

He is a good cricketer
A cricketer is a man

to

He is a man better than most cricketers

but this conclusion does not follow, and is just as objectionable as the original one, 'He is a good man'. We should get nearer to an acceptable conclusion only with something like

He is a man better at cricket (*or* better as a cricketer) than most cricketers

41

and even this is dubious, since there seems no contradiction in the idea that, so flourishing is the state of the game, most cricketers are pretty good; if this is possible, the comparative analysis in anything like its present form disappears altogether. But apart from that, the comparative analysis in any case has not unstuck 'good' from its substantive; in the conclusion above, the connection persists, with 'good' now in its comparative form. So the attributiveness of 'good' demands a more intimate connection with its substantive than is demanded in the case of a merely comparative adjective like 'large'.

Since 'good' in this sort of construction is intimately connected with the substantive that it qualifies, the meaning of a phrase of the form 'a good x' has to be taken as a whole; and its meaning is partly determined by what fills the place of 'x'. Can we go further than this and say that in phrases of this form, the meaning of the whole is *essentially* determined by the meaning of what takes the place of 'x'? In many cases, it looks as though we might take this further step. For if we consider functional descriptions of artefacts, such as 'clock' or 'tin opener', or again descriptions of human beings which refer to their roles or jobs or skilled activities, such as 'gardener' or 'general' or 'cricketer', it does seem that if one understands these expressions (at least in the strong sense that one understands what a tin opener is, for instance, or what a general does), then one has understanding, within limits, of what a good thing of that sort is.

This understanding may be at a very general and abstract level and there will be a lot of room for disagreement, and for sophisticated comparisons of merits, within the broad and abstract framework. In particular, there can be differing or changing views of what aspects of a human activity are to have what sort of weight in the evaluation: thus one person, or one age, may take a different view from another about how important it is for a good general to gain his victories at a minimum loss of life. Nevertheless, an understanding of what an x is does seem, in these cases, to contain a general understanding of the criteria appropriate to saying that something is a good x: we are not just free to invent criteria of goodness. The clearest cases of all are, of course, those of technical descriptions of artefacts; if someone went into an aircraft factory and said 'that's a good aerofoil', with reference to a rejected prototype which was in fact ill-designed or ill-executed, he would just have made a mistake; and if he then explained that he said this because its shape or its polish took his fancy, this would not make his remark any better, because these are not criteria of being *a good aerofoil*, though they may well be appropriate to some other evaluation of this piece of metal, for instance as an aesthetic object. (This illustrates once more the importance, with evaluation, of the question, under what concept is the thing being evaluated.)

There is a powerful tradition in contemporary philosophy of resistance to the idea that criteria of value, what makes a thing of a certain sort a good thing of that sort, could ever be logically determined by factual or conceptual truths: this is a central application of the distinction between fact and value which we have already referred to. This resistance was influentially encouraged by Moore, who invented the phrase 'the naturalistic fallacy' for a mistake allegedly committed by any view which held that the goodness of a thing could be identified with some set of empirical, or indeed metaphysical, characteristics. Moore exposed this mistake in terms of his own view that goodness was a nonnatural property, a view which we have already seen to be, in so far as it is comprehensible at all, a sad error. Many modern philosophers who agree that Moore was in error in that view, nevertheless agree with him that 'the naturalistic fallacy' is a genuine and important fallacy; they give a new explanation of its nature. This explanation, crudely put, comes to something like this: that the function of statements of the form 'that is a good x' is to prescribe or commend, or to perform some such linguistic purpose in the general range of the normative or evaluative, whereas merely to describe the characteristics of x is not to perform such a purpose; and no set of statements which do not perform such a purpose can logically entail any statement which does. To prescribe, commend, etc., is to do something, which (to put it roughly) the facts by themselves cannot make us do; we must have some evaluative or prescriptive attitude which favours certain characteristics, if those characteristics are to count with us as grounds of approval. Merely knowing about the world, or understanding concepts, cannot in itself be enough to bring this about.

A full examination of this position requires something that would take us too far in this essay, an enquiry into an important and developing field in the philosophy of language, the theory of *speech-acts*, the various things that we can do by making utterances. Three points can be briefly made. First, there cannot be any very simple connection between speech-acts such as commending or prescribing on the one hand, and the meaning of sentences such as 'this is a good x' on the other. At best, the utterance of those sentences will constitute an act of commendation, etc., only if the sentences are actually *asserted*; but the sentence has the same meaning whether it is asserted or not. Thus we understand the sentence 'This is a good film' in the context 'If this is a good film, it will get an Oscar'; but in that context it is not asserted, and no actual act of commendation has occurred.* Thus the connection between meaning and commendation must at least be indirect.

Second, the theory seems too readily to assume that the functions of commending, etc., and of describing, are exclusive of one another. Yet one and the same utterance may carry many speech-acts at once: if I say 'Tomorrow will be wet', I may at once have described tomorrow's weather, made a prediction, given you a warning, etc. Further, the question of whether I do, in making a certain utterance, perform any of these speech-acts, may be determined by what I say together with the facts of the situation. Thus if I say 'The ice is thin', I will have described the ice, no doubt, but also, in the light merely of your interests and purposes, may have done something that counts as giving you a warning. Rather similarly (though not exactly similarly), if I say, in a description of this clock, that it keeps the time exactly, needs no winding, never breaks down, etc., I will have done something like commending it as a clock quite independently of some supposed choice of criteria for clocks on my part. Of course, the

*See J. R. Searle, 'Meaning and Speech-Acts', *Philosophical Review*, Vol. 71 (1962), and *Speech Acts* (Cambridge University Press, 1969), Chapter 6.

facts about this clock, and the general nature of clocks, cannot bring it about that I make the remark – I may remain silent: but they determine that *if* I give a true description of this clock in these respects, then I do something in the range of commending or giving a favourable evaluation of the clock.

This last point brings us to the third consideration. Activities such as commending, etc., are essentially overt activities, connected with actual utterances; this is why I have said that their study belongs to the theory of speech-acts. But no account of sentences containing 'good' could possibly be adequate which remained merely at this level; for it is possible merely to think, or believe, or reach the conclusion that something is good of its sort, without making an utterance to that effect at all. Hating Bloggs, I may carefully refrain from making favourable remarks about his performance as a cricketer, i.e., precisely not commend him or do any such thing; yet in my thought I may be forced to recognize that he is a good cricketer. An adequate account must leave room for such recognition.

These extremely sketchy considerations may indicate some difficulties in the revamped version of the rejection of the 'naturalistic fallacy'. I think, in fact, that as a general doctrine about the workings of 'good' the harsh distinction between fact and value that goes with that view is mistaken: it seems clear that for many fillings of '*x*' in 'that is a good *x*', an understanding of what an *x* is or does, and factual knowledge about this *x* – i.e., a combination of conceptual and factual information – is sufficient for one to determine, at least broadly, the truth or falsity of the judgement. This, certainly, is objectivity. But is it so for all fillings of '*x*'?

When we examine this question, we find cases where the going is much harder, and where the fact/value distinction, or something like it, gets a better grip: where some deeper considerations about value emerge. What much contemporary philosophy has presented as a very general logical doctrine about the workings of 'good' may be seen to have its interest rather as a much more restricted, and not purely logical, doctrine about the goodness of things and, more particularly, persons, under certain specific descriptions.

GOODNESS AND ROLES

CONSIDER the expression 'a good father'.* While it is moderately clear in outline what sort of criteria go with this expression, it is not at all clear that an understanding of these is involved in understanding what it is to be a father. Nor is this merely because the idea of being a good father contains a reference to certain social conventions; for so, indeed, does 'cricketer' or 'bank clerk' – to know what a bank clerk is involves knowing a good deal about the social fabric in terms of which the role of a bank clerk is defined – but when I understand that role in those terms, I also understand in outline the sorts of things that a man would have to do in order to be called a good bank clerk. The difference with the idea of a good father is that it looks as though one can have a perfectly clear idea of fatherhood, and this not in itself lead one to an understanding of the sorts of things that make someone a good father. The explanation of this difference lies partly in the fact that the idea of fatherhood which we can grasp without grasping the evaluative criteria is an idea of fatherhood merely as a biological relationship; but it cannot be merely *that* idea which occurs in the notion of a good father. If we have in mind the idea of a father only as a procreator, it is not clear what we could even mean by calling someone 'a good

* See G. Cohen, 'Beliefs and Roles', *Proceedings of the Aristotelian Society*, Vol. 67 (1966–7).

father' – unless we meant that he was good at becoming a father.

Nor do we necessarily advance towards evaluative notions merely by introducing a reference to social institutions such as marriage. 'Wife's brother' is a well-defined kinship relation, involving a reference to marriage, but the idea of being a good wife's brother is one which, in our society, lacks any content. The content of 'a good father' is determined by the biological relationship together with certain responsibilities which, in our sort of society, are ascribed to people in that relationship. Only when there are such responsibilities can we say that 'father' refers not merely to a biological relationship, but to a role; and the role can, of course, exceptionally be played by someone not in the biological relationship, as when someone is said to have been a father to an orphaned child. The difference from 'bank clerk' then emerges in this: that there is no notion of 'bank clerk' which does not involve a reference to the responsibilities, and the term refers to a role which can only be explained in relation to social institutions which give someone with that role certain functions and duties. Whereas under the role-concept of fatherhood there lies the more restricted concept of it as a purely natural relationship, a relationship which in our sort of society is taken as the basis of that sort of role.

If a man is an ardent cricketer and perhaps has entered cricketing as a profession, then his performance as a cricketer and assessments of that performance by the competent, will obviously matter to him; if he does poorly, he has failed. A man who modestly plays some part on the cricket field on a Sunday afternoon will, equally obviously, tend to care less; the evident truth that he is a poor cricketer means little to him – he might say that he wasn't a cricketer but merely someone who occasionally played cricket. A man who was a very indifferent bank clerk, doing barely what was expected of him, might equally, though in a rather different way, have dissociated himself from doing well in those activities. He may hate the bank, despise banking, and care only about his friends and growing chrysanthemums. The bank he regards only as the means to a living; he does not, in any important sense, see himself as a bank clerk. Yet he could hardly say that he *wasn't* a bank clerk (really), or if he did, he might be in danger of retreating into fantasy; for too much of his life is in fact bound up with this role which, like it or not, he has. The unfavourable attitudes and lack of respect which he encounters from his superiors in the bank, while he may have succeeded in caring little for them, he at any rate cannot dismiss (as the cricketing man can) as based on a misunderstanding: the contractual relationship of his job puts him in a position where this is what he must expect. Though he may have reached stability in this situation, by irony perhaps, the situation is not a happy one, and if he came into money he might well (if it did not now require too much courage) get rid of the role and resign from the bank.

Contrast with these simple prototypes, another – that of the unwilling drafted soldier. His life, very probably more miserable than that of the bank clerk, *could* involve a yet more uneasy and ambiguous state of mind – if, for instance, he was just unsure whether, being a soldier, he should try to put up a good performance as a soldier. But his state of mind could be simpler than this if he straightforwardly thought that 'soldier' was a title that applied to him only because it had been forcibly applied to him from the outside; cared nothing for the assessments that go with that title; regarded the hostility of his superiors as a blank external force like the force that had put him into the army; and felt as the only constraint on opting out as much as possible, the fear of punishment. The straightforwardness of this attitude may be bought at the cost of a certain despair, since it naturally goes with a feeling (as in *Catch* 22) that the environment is, just as a matter of brute fact, insane.

In other cases, a man may come to dissociate himself from a role and the assessments that apply to it, with which previously he has wholeheartedly or unreflectingly identified himself, because he cannot bring himself to do something which he is expected to do in that role. In favourable circumstances, he may be able to resign from it. If that is not possible, he may feel required to refrain in some other way from doing what would be expected of someone in his role: in an extreme political case, possibly by covert disobedience and subversion. It is said of certain German generals who during the war were appalled by Hitler's policies that they were for a long time inhibited from setting to work against him by considerations of the oath they had taken, as officers of the Wehrmacht, to obey him. One might wonder, from outside the situation, how any oath taken to that man who was then in that condition and ruling by those means could have been regarded as inextricably bound up with one's duties even *as a German officer* – this is to regard oaths as having, not just sanctity, but magical powers. But suppose obedience to the oath could be established as certainly part of one's duties as a German officer; then what the generals needed was to form the conception of things they had to do which were contrary to what they were supposed to do as German officers – that is to say, it was no longer under the title, and in the role, of *German officer* that they had to act. And this was a conception which, it seems, some of them found it very difficult to form. For them, 'a German officer' was not just something that they were, but what they were.

These schematic examples are supposed to illustrate ways in which men may dissociate themselves from roles which they bear, roles which bring with them certain sorts of assessment of their activities. This dissociation may be, in different cases, variously defensible or indefensible, noble or ignoble, prudent or the reverse; but it is in every case intelligible, and it is comprehensible how a man can form a coherent picture of himself in relation to a role which he has or used to have or might be thought to have, in which he does not allow the standards that go with that role to be ultimate, basic, or important in the assessment of the success or excellence of his life. Now this possibility seems to me a vital counterbalance to a fact which we have already noticed, namely that these various sorts of title and role can conceptually carry with them broad standards of assessment of people under those titles, as the descriptions of artefacts can carry standards of assessment of those artefacts. While the standards can be in this way logically welded to the title, the title is not logically welded to the man; hence the standards are not logically welded to the man. Through his consciousness of a given title and his relation to it, a man may refuse to make those standards the determinants of his life.

It does not follow from these possibilities that someone who unreflectively and passively leads a life structured by some role which he takes for granted must in fact have *chosen* that role, as Sartre (some of whose concerns are mirrored in these remarks) seems, in his classical Existentialist period, to have thought. Hence his description of an unreflective condition of this sort as a condition of *bad faith*. This requires at least that every man has the possibility of reflection and choice, and that this possibility is both recognized and renounced. Yet even the first step, of a real possibility of reflection and choice, may be too much to ascribe to men in some social and psychological situations. Sartre's view is connected with his extremely nonempirical notion of freedom, a notion which may also help to explain a certain ambiguity in his thought between the ideas that man has no essence, and that man has an essence, which is freedom.

If there were some title or role with which standards were necessarily connected and which, by necessity, a man could not fail to have nor dissociate himself from, then there would be some standards which a man would have to recognize as determinants of his life, at least on pain of failing to have any consciousness at all of what he was. There is certainly one 'title' – for good reason, we can scarcely speak here of a 'role' – which is necessarily inalienable, and that is the title of 'man' itself. So it is a central question whether 'man' is a concept which itself provides standards of assessment and excellence as a man; for if it does, then it seems that they *must* be our standards.

There have famously been philosophies which have held that it did: that either directly, by reflection on the concept of 'man', or more indirectly, by reflection on some supposed further necessary truths about what man is, one could arrive at an understanding of what a good man must be.

Such philosophies can helpfully be distinguished, at least initially, into two sorts – those that do, and those that do not, make a transcendental appeal, that is to say, an appeal to some framework for human life which lies outside human life and the empirical world. We may start with the nontranscendental type and come later to an example (a religious example) of the transcendental type.

MORAL STANDARDS AND THE
DISTINGUISHING MARK OF MAN

A PROTOTYPE of the nontranscendental type is to be found in the philosophy of Aristotle. According to Aristotle, there are certain characteristics, in particular, certain activities and powers, which are distinctive of man, and the life of the good man will exemplify to the fullest degree the development of those powers and activities. Or, more accurately, there is one distinctive feature of man – his ability to shape his actions and dispositions by reason – which will be manifested in the *highest* degree; other of his potentialities will, under the ordering power of reason, be realized in a balanced way and not each maximally. Practical reason is supposed to produce coherence, and reduce conflict, among the desires of the individual living (as man must live) in society. This aim of reducing conflict between desires, while not inordinately suppressing them, is part of what gives recognizable content to the claim that the aim of the sort of life outlined in Aristotle's system is *happiness*.

The importance of the harmonization of desires in Aristotle, and of practical reason in securing this, is illustrated in a backhanded way by his notable failure to deal with one problem of reconciliation which, in his own terms, must be important. The 'reason' that we have so far referred to is *practical* reason, which applies to particular actions and desires and which is the ground of what Aristotle (or rather his translators) call 'virtues of character' – that is to say, those dispositions to right action which involve motivations of pleasure and pain. There is also, however, *theoretical* reason, the power of thinking correctly about abstract questions of science and philosophy, which Aristotle is disposed to regard as a yet higher expression of man's nature: the most excellent form of human life, accordingly, is one devoted in fair degree to intellectual enquiry. He makes it clear that since man is man, and not a god, his life cannot solely be devoted to this, and he must also have a life to which the virtues of character are necessary.

What Aristotle does not do, however – and granted his system, cannot do – is to provide any account of how the intellectual activities, the highest expression (in his view) of man's nature, are to be brought into relation to the citizenly activities which are regulated by the virtues of character. Practical wisdom does not stretch so far and could not impose a 'mean' between philosophizing or doing science on the one hand and being a good citizen, father, etc., on the other. It is a curious, and significant, feature of Aristotle's system that the highest potentialities of man have admittedly to compete with others for expression, but no coherent account can be given of how this competition is to be regulated.

This is one weakness of Aristotle's attempt to elicit the good for man out of man's nature by appealing to a distinguishing mark of man, his intelligence and capacity for rational thought: a weakness that can be seen in the following light, that the pure or creative aspects of intelligence would seem to be the highest form of these capacities, yet a total commitment to

their expression is ruled out, and a less than total commitment is not represented as something that practical
thought can rationally arrive at. This weakness in
Aristotle's system is a model of a more general problem: what might possibly be called the 'Gauguin problem', except that that label imports rather special and
Romantic connotations of the claims of *self*-expression. A moralist who wants to base a conception of the
right sort of life for man on considerations about the
high and distinctive powers of man can scarcely disregard the claims of creative genius in the arts or
sciences to be included pre-eminently among such powers; yet he will find it hard to elicit from, or even reconcile with, an ideal of the development and expression
of such genius, many of the virtues and commitments
which belong to morality, some of which are merely
more everyday, while most make demands on one's relations to other people which are quite different from
those made by creative work.

Plato, it must be said, saw one half of this problem
with extreme clarity. The famous banishment of all but
celebratory art from his *Republic* (a state designed precisely as an institutionalization of morality) was the
product of his taking art seriously and his seeing perfectly correctly that both the life of the creative artist
and the effects on a serious public of the free exploration embodied in his creations were likely to resist the
demands of stability made by the fully moralized society. We may well reject the alternative Plato chose, but
he was surely right in seeing these as alternatives: a
society protected against moral and social change, and a
society in which free creation and exploration through
art is permitted. The reason why (as I put it) he saw only

one half of this problem is that he did permit, indeed made the central activity of his ruling class, creative intellectual activity – and one may well wonder whether this would have proved any more compatible in the long run with the kind of stability he longed for. (It seems that he admired the intellectual achievements of Athens while deploring its political and moral disorder, and admired the political stability of Sparta while regretting its unintellectual militarism. It must surely have occurred to him to wonder whether it was just an accident that these qualities were distributed as they were.) Part of the explanation is that where we speak of 'creative activity', Plato thought largely in terms of discovery: the philosophical activity was in his view inherently disciplined by the *a priori* moral truths waiting to be discovered. If we reject this picture of moral philosophy and admit further that in natural science there is an ineliminable creative element, these intellectual activities will look less like natural inhabitants of the kind of environment which Plato provided for them.

I am not saying (what seems to me high-minded nonsense) that the very activities of scientific enquiry require or presuppose that persons engaged in such enquiry will have liberal and humane values, opposed to an authoritarian social environment. Recent experience suggests that the most that such enquiries presuppose is a certain liberalism in the environment of science itself, which can well coexist with a cynical indifference to many humane considerations, concerning (for instance) how scientific discoveries are employed or the source of funds which support the research. But this itself is only another illustration of the various ways in which demands of morality can

58

conflict with the unimpeded development of human creative and intellectual aspirations; it is, for us, much too late in the day to say that because natural science clearly constitutes one of the highest achievements of men, its development must have an unchallengeable claim on our moral approval. It would be as optimistic for us to think this, as it was for Plato to think that the pursuit of these activities could coexist with the degree of social restriction and illiberalism which *he* identified with the moralized society.

This illustrates one, rather central, objection to the Aristotelian enterprise, with reference to the particular (and plausible) selection of intellect as the distinguishing mark. There are more general objections to the procedure of trying to elicit unquestionable moral ends or ideals from distinguishing marks of man's nature. We may mention three. First, a palpable degree of evaluation has already gone into the selection of the distinguishing mark which is given this role, such as rationality or creativity. If one approached without preconceptions the question of finding characteristics which differentiate men from other animals, one could as well, on these principles, end up with a morality which exhorted men to spend as much time as possible in making fire; or developing peculiarly human physical characteristics; or having sexual intercourse without regard to season; or despoiling the environment and upsetting the balance of nature; or killing things for fun.

Second, and very basically, this approach bears out the moral *ambiguity* of distinctive human characteristics (though Aristotle paid some attention, not totally successfully, to this point). For if it is a mark of a man

59

to employ intelligence and tools in modifying his environment, it is equally a mark of him to employ intelligence in getting his own way and tools in destroying others. If it is a mark of a man to have a conceptualized and fully conscious awareness of himself as one among others, aware that others have feelings like himself, this is a precondition not only of benevolence but (as Nietzsche pointed out) of cruelty as well: the man of sadistic sophistication is not more like other animals than the man of natural affections, but less so. If we offer as the supreme moral imperative that old cry, 'be a man!', it is terrible to think of many of the ways in which it could be taken literally.

Here we seem to encounter a genuine dimension of freedom, to use or neglect the natural endowment, and to use it in one way or another: a freedom which must cut the central cord of the Aristotelian sort of enterprise. Nor can this freedom itself be used as the distinguishing mark of man, and the enterprise mounted again on the basis of that. For this freedom can surely, by its nature, determine no one form of life as against another – as Sartre, in virtue of a central ambiguity already mentioned, perhaps has thought. One might say: if there were a distinctive form of life, that of 'realizing freedom', then there must still be a freedom to reject that, too.

Third, if we revert to that particular case of the *rational* as the distinguishing mark of man: there is a tendency for this approach to acquire a Manichean leaning and emphasize virtues of rational self-control at the expense of all else. There is no reason why such an outlook should *inevitably* follow; apart from anything else, it involves a false and inhuman view of the passions themselves as blind causal forces or merely animal characteristics. To be helplessly in love is in fact as distinctively a human condition as to approve rationally of someone's moral dispositions. But it is easy to see why, in the present direction, Manicheanism looks inviting. If rationality and consistent thought are the preferred distinguishing marks of man, then even if it is admitted that man, as a whole, also has passions, the supremacy of rational thought over them may well seem an unquestionable idea'. This is all the more so, since it is quite obvious that gaining some such control is a basic condition of growing up, and even, at the extreme, of sanity. But to move from that into making such control into *the* ideal, rules out *a priori* most forms of spontaneity. And this seems to be absurd.

All these considerations suggest that the attempt to found morality on a conception of the *good man* elicited from considerations of the distinguishing marks of human nature is likely to fail. I am far from thinking that considerations about human nature, what men are, what it is for men to live in society, do not contribute to a correct view of morality. Of course they do: one could not have any conception of morality at all without such considerations. In particular, they help to delimit the possible content of what could be regarded as a morality. Just as obviously, differing views of human nature (as, for example, some psychoanalytical view) must have differing effects on what views one takes of particular moral requirements and norms. Not merely scientific or semi-scientific views must have this effect but also views in the philosophy of mind. Thus a proper philosophical understanding of the nature of the emotions should have a discouraging

61

effect on Manichean views about their management, and philosophical considerations about the nature, indeed the existence, of something called the *will* must have a direct effect on moralities which find in the exercise of the will (against the desires, for instance) a central clue to moral worth.

While all this is true, and while there are very definite limitations on what could be comprehensibly regarded as a system of human morality, there is no direct route from considerations of human nature to a unique morality and a unique moral ideal. It would be simpler if there were fewer things, and fewer distinctively human things, that men can be; or if the characters, dispositions, social arrangements and states of affairs which men can comprehensibly set value on were all, in full development, consistent with one another. But they are not, and there is good reason why they are not: good reason which itself emerges from considerations of human nature.

GOD, MORALITY, AND PRUDENCE

WE distinguished some time ago among views which seek to elicit a notion of a good man from considerations of human nature – those that set man in some transcendental framework and those that did not. Having just said something about the second sort, I shall now turn to look at an example of the first. In the course of doing this, it will be helpful to discuss a question which is important apart from the present issue – the relations of the moral and the prudential.

A leading feature of this sort of theory is that it seeks to provide, in terms of the transcendental framework, something that man is *for*: if he understands properly his role in the basic scheme of things, he will see that there are some particular sorts of ends which are properly his and which he ought to realize. One archetypal form of such a view is the belief that man was created by a God who also has certain expectations of him.

A central difficulty with this lies in the question of which properties of God are supposed to justify the claim that we ought to satisfy his expectations. If it is his power, or the mere fact that he created us, analogies with human kings or fathers (often employed in this connection) leave us with the recognition that there are many kings and fathers who ought not to be obeyed. If it is urged that God has infinite power and created everything, we point out that infinite kinghood or creatordom does not seem evidently more worthy of obedience but merely more difficult to disobey. If it is then said that in addition to these other properties God is good, the objection is forthcoming (as it was from Kant) that this already involves a recognition of what is admirable and valuable, a recognition of the kind which the appeal to God was supposed to underwrite.

Such arguments, which are very familiar, may be taken as attacking the idea that one might work out purely deductively and *a priori* the required life for man from a description of him as *created by God*. In that role, they seem to me successful. But such arguments tend to carry with them a larger ambition – to show that even if God's existence were established, that fact could not in principle supply any acceptable or appropriate *motive* for moral conduct, of a kind which would otherwise be lacking. In this role, too, the arguments are very widely accepted, so that it is practically a philosophers' platitude that even if God did exist, that would not, to a clear-headed and moral thinker, make any difference to the situation of morality. The origins of this view go back to a famous discussion in Plato's *Euthyphro*, but in its modern form it owes most to Kant. It owes to him in particular a clear statement of the assumptions on which it rests – assumptions about the essential *purity* of moral motivation. These assumptions are pervasive in much moral thought, and their influence and importance goes a long way beyond the present issue of a religious morality. They are also very importantly mistaken.

The argument, in simplest form, goes something like this. Either one's motives for following the moral word of God are moral motives, or they are not. If they are, then one is already equipped with moral motivations, and the introduction of God adds nothing extra. But if they are not moral motives, then they will be motives of such a kind that they cannot appropriately motivate *morality* at all: in particular, they are likely to be motives of prudence, a possibility most crudely portrayed by certain evangelists (whether of belief or disbelief) in terms of hellfire. But nothing motivated by prudential considerations can be genuinely moral action; genuinely moral action must be motivated by the consideration that it is morally right and by no other consideration at all. So, taking this all together, we reach the conclusion that any appeal to God in this connection either adds nothing at all, or it adds the wrong sort of thing.

Two questions are raised about morality and motivation by this sort of argument. First, whether there are really no relevant types of motivation except moral or prudential – that is to say, whether the distinction between moral and prudential is exhaustive. Second, whether a policy or outlook may not be moral, while being in some way at the same time prudential – that is to say, whether the distinction is exclusive. Let us take the second question first. Is it essential to morality to distinguish totally the moral and the prudential?

Here we need to make some distinctions. It is certainly true that it is essential to morality that a distinction is drawn *at some level* between the moral and the prudential. At the most primitive level, it is clear that any morality has to apply this distinction, or something like it, to actions and policies; it has to be able to distinguish actions and policies which are *selfish* and which minister to the gratification or safety of the agent at the expense of others, from those which take the interests of others into account. If some such distinction is not made, there are no moral considerations, at all. It is clear that the religious morality we are discussing, however crudely put, can observe this distinction at the primitive level: it will, with respect to the secular world, approve policies and actions which take the interests of others into account and will disapprove selfish policies.

However, it may be thought that this level of drawing the distinction is, by itself, too primitive, and that we need to extend the distinction from merely classifying policies and intentional actions, to discriminating between motives. Thus one who gives money to charity merely to improve his reputation with the Rotary Club or to ease his own guilt, acts no more morally than if he had spent the money on his own pleasures. (The example illustrates why it was appropriate to speak of 'intentional action' and to distinguish this from the question of motive. The self-interested business man who writes a cheque to famine relief, does so intentionally, and his intention is that the money should go to famine relief: if famine is relieved by his action, this will not be, relative to his thoughts in so acting, an *accident*. The point is that his motive was not a concern for the relief of famine, but for his own reputation or comfort.)

If we say, as many would say, that the man who so acts acts no more morally than one who spends the money on himself, it will not follow that what he does is no better than what is done by the simply selfish man; for famine will be, hopefully, relieved, and this is better than that another combined cocktail cabinet and TV set should be bought. Nor, surely, can it follow that we merely approve of the act and do not in *any* sense approve of the agent; for we can say of him that he has intentionally done something which it is a good thing to have done, and this surely constitutes some sort of approval, if a limited sort, of him. The point, presumably, is that we do not *morally* approve of him. There is a very good point in saying this, but it must not be taken too far. For if we insist that to act morally is essentially to act from a moral motivation, we may well be tempted to add to that the innocuous-looking proposition that all that can matter from a moral point of view is that people should act morally, and then conclude (rightly, from those premises) that from the moral point of view any two situations of self-interested motivation are indistinguishable, and it must be impossible from the moral point of view to prefer one to the other. This is absurd. It is not perhaps logically absurd, but morally absurd – the Puritan moral absurdity that the only morally relevant property of the world is how much righteousness it contains. But since this is morally absurd (or, rather, since it is obviously not incoherent to regard it as morally absurd), it follows that something else *is* logically absurd: namely a view of morality from which it follows that that is the only moral position which is coherently tenable.

What is, then, the point and content of saying that we do not *morally* approve of the self-interested donor to charity, or that, though he does a good thing, he does not act morally? With what motivations, first, are we contrasting this man's motivation? Some, such as Kant and R. M. Hare, have laid emphasis on the contrast with acting *from principle*; roughly, doing it just because one thinks one ought to. Others, such as Hume, have emphasized the contrast with doing something because one cares disinterestedly about the situation which one's action is supposed to alter or cares about the other people involved. Leaving aside the notable differences between these two formulations, they do have something in common: that the man who has a moral motivation for doing things of the non-self-regarding sort, has a disposition or general motive for doing things of that sort; whereas the self-interested man has no such steady motive, for it will always only be luck if what benefits others happens to coincide with what, by the limited criteria of simple self-interest, happens to benefit him. This must surely, as Hume said, have something to do with the *point* of selecting certain motives for *moral* approbation: we are concerned to have people who have a general tendency to be prepared to consider other people's interests on the same footing as their own, and if necessary to put other people's interests first.

It is perhaps worth noting, in passing, that one of the (numerous) advantages of Hume's emphasis in this matter, with its stress on sympathy and feeling for other people's situation, as opposed to the Kantian emphasis on acting from principle, is that it introduces a similarity between the sorts of reasons one has for doing things for others, and the sorts of reasons one has for doing them for oneself. Despite the mechanical character of Hume's psychological system, it makes some sense of the idea that to care about others' pain is an extension of caring about one's own: the second is indeed a necessary condition of the first, and there is certainly no problem (as there should not be) about why a man who is concerned about others may not also be reasonably concerned about himself. Under the Kantian emphasis, however, this suddenly emerges as a problem, since to act with regard to one's own interests, in a straightforward way, is to act from a kind of motive which has nothing to do with morality at all and is indeed alien to it. Since we are presumably enjoined to maximize moral action, extremes of self-denial would seem to follow, as derived, indeed, from the concept of morality itself. At the best, doing what one simply wants to do will constitute unregulated and probably guilty departures from the moral point of view. To cope with this problem, the Kantian tradition produces a set of 'duties to oneself', recognition of which licenses one to do for moral reasons some of the things one would be disposed to do anyway. This absurd apparatus is just the product of trying to adjust to some rather more reasonable view of human life the awkward consequences of holding three things – that morality is concerned above all with motivation, that moral motivation is motivation of principle, and that the moral point of view must be ubiquitous. To avoid these particular awkward consequences, it would be enough to abandon any one of these propositions; but there are good reasons for abandoning all of them.

To revert, after this diversion, to our religious moralist. We saw that he could quite easily draw a distinction, though a primitive one, between the moral and the prudential. I think that we can see now that he can even draw a more refined distinction, at the level of motivation. It was suggested that one (though perhaps not the only) point of distinguishing between moral and self-interested motivations was that of picking out general dispositions to do things of the non-self-interested sort. But dispositions of this sort, the man with even a crude religious morality will certainly admit. Indeed, perhaps what his God wants is that men should feel for the sufferings of each other and act in one another's interests because they so feel. So a lot of the time persons of this belief, if they did as God would like them to, would act from ordinary human motives which by most people (other than Kantians) would be regarded as themselves moral motives. If these fail, or temptation to selfish action is strong, then perhaps the crude believer's thoughts turn a while to hellfire, and this fortifies a disposition to do things of the non-self-interested sort (in the worldly sense of 'self-interest', that is). While his action is in this sense prudential, it is not prudential in that sense in which it is essential to the concept of morality that the prudential be contrasted with the moral. Indeed, there is a special reason why his actions, though prudential, are not selfish: namely there is presumably no effective way of aiming at salvation *at the expense of others*.

In fact, it is quite unrealistic to force onto our religious moralist (or anyone else) an exhaustive disjunction between the prudential and the moral. Leaving aside the more general operations of sympathy of which Hume wrote: what about someone who does something in the interests of another, and to his own disadvantage, because he loves that person; or, indeed, is in love with them; or admires them; or respects them; or because they are (after all) a member of the family? None of these reasons for acting have to be moral reasons, in any exigent or purified sense of that term; equally they are not prudential reasons. Nor, again, do they belong to the third class of motive moral philosophy has sometimes allowed, that of *inclination*, that is, doing something because you feel like doing it. Clearly the list of examples could be extended indefinitely to include vast numbers of the special relationships in which one person can stand to another. It is a grotesque product of theory and strenuous moralism to suppose that 'moral' and 'prudential' sufficiently divide up the justifiable motives or reasons a man can have for doing something: they leave out, in fact, almost everything. We do need something over and above these particular, or more specific, motivations, just because they are particular and specific, and especially because the particular relationship I have to another person may be of a hostile character, and there will in all probability be no other, more beneficent, particular relationship in the offing to inhibit destructive conduct. So of course we need, over and above, general motivations to control and regulate these particular ones; and the most general thing that is over and above is morality. But, happily for humanity, we do not have to leave it to those general considerations to motivate everything of a desirable kind. Some of our decent actions come not from that motive which Christians misrepresent as our loving everybody, but just from our loving somebody.

The religious moralist, now, can see the general requirements as stemming from a particular relation, that to God, and this relation can be represented as one of love, or awe, or respect, or whatever words are found appropriate for this baffling semantic task. And this relation he will rightly resist being categorized as either moral or prudential in its practical import. I think, however, that he may have to be careful about saying that this is an attitude towards God which anyone who

71

knows what God is *ought* to have, for this might, in the way that Kant insisted on, make morality prior to God again. He will have to say, rather, that this is an attitude which anyone who knows what God is will inevitably have; God is one whose word exacts an unquestioning acceptance. In itself, this is still not enough, of course; compatibly with this much, God could be an unfailing hypnotist. So the believer will proceed, as always, by negation and analogy and say that it is not like that, but *more* like a loving father, and so forth. I myself doubt whether at the end he will produce any coherent account at all. But this is because of difficulties in belief in God, not because of something in the nature of morality. I do not think it right – and these arguments have been trying to show this – to say, as many do, that even if God existed, this could give no special and acceptable reason for subscribing to morality. If God existed, there might well be special, and acceptable, reasons for subscribing to morality. The trouble is that the attempt to formulate those reasons in better than the crudest outline runs into the impossibility of thinking coherently about God. The trouble with religious morality comes not from morality's being inescapably pure, but from religion's being incurably unintelligible.

WHAT IS MORALITY ABOUT?

THIS last discussion has led us sideways into certain questions of what morality is about and how 'the moral' is to be delimited. A lot has been written about this, in search of some criteria for distinguishing the moral from the non-moral. These recent discussions are considered by G. J. Warnock in his admirably concise, lucid, and forceful book *Contemporary Moral Philosophy*:* he rightly emphasizes the extraordinary fact that a great deal of this discussion has proceeded in a vacuum, in pursuit of a criterion which might give us *a* way of distinguishing moral and non-moral, perhaps a way which bore some rough resemblance to ways in which we, now, make such a distinction, but without shedding any light on, or being guided by, the evidently more basic question of what this distinction is *for*, what significant point is made by dividing up human actions, or policies, or motives, or reasons along these lines. Some of the remarks in the previous section touch on that point.

I shall assume as given – indeed I have already assumed it earlier – a conclusion which Mr Warnock reaches in his discussion and which must certainly be correct, namely that any significant delimitation of the moral must involve reference to the *content* of the judgements, policies, principles, or whatever, that are being described as 'moral'. It might perhaps surprise people innocent of moral philosophy that anyone has

*Macmillan, 1967.

73

ever supposed this not to be so; but it has in fact been maintained, and frequently, that moral views (as opposed to non-moral ones) can be identified without reference to their content, by some considerations such as their being practical maxims which are entirely universal or their being practical maxims which are acknowledged as overriding other practical maxims. The motive for these improbable manoeuvres has been, as always, the maintenance of the fact/value distinction. For suppose one introduces a reference to the content of the moral and says (for instance) that moral views essentially refer to human well-being, where 'well-being' has itself some content and does not merely mean 'whatever one thinks ought to happen to human beings': then the range of possible moral views is seriously limited by facts and by logic, contrary to the fact/value distinction. This motive for the manoeuvres hardly makes them any more attractive than do their consequences.

The question I want to discuss here is not, then, this general point, but the merits of the partial criterion I just mentioned, of a reference to human well-being as a mark of a moral position; advanced by Mrs P. R. Foot and others, this proposal is itself well regarded by Mr Warnock. If this is to be defended, it is essential both that the test be applied at a very general level and that 'well-being' be interpreted in a very general way – though not, of course, in such a general way that it becomes vacuous.

The first point comes out in this, that certainly one could not apply such a test to the motivation of *particular actions*, and always get the right results: it must rather be that if one's approval of such more general things as policies, institutions, dispositions, sorts of motive, etc., is to count as moral approval, then one must suppose that those policies, institutions, etc., minister in some way to the achievement of some kind of human well-being. The second point is that 'well-being' certainly cannot be interpreted, for these purposes, as meaning merely that the persons involved in these situations get what they actually want nor (what is not necessarily the same thing) that they enjoy the outcome. For it must surely be possible to recognize as moral views (though utilitarians will be disposed to think that they are mistaken moral views) outlooks which hold that people very often want and enjoy the wrong things.

Nor – though this is more contestable – is it clear that 'well-being' in this connection can be identified with *happiness*. Certainly if we think (as the English language, as it now is, rather encourages us to think) that *contentment* is a sufficient, though not a necessary, condition of happiness, it will not do for the present purpose; we must be able to recognize as moral views (though cynics will think them mistaken) outlooks which deplore contentment, if secured at too low a level of consciousness and activity. Even if we break this connection and refuse to count as 'happy' those who are content in some bovine, doped, or subdued state – as Aristotle and, with noble inconsistency, J. S. Mill, refused to count them – and insist on a more activist or reflective level of happiness, it is still not clear that we have what the thesis requires. The idea of a man's being happy, and indeed the less episodic notion of his being *a happy man*, has surely *something* to do with his not suffering; or his not suffering too much;

or at the limit, not suffering in the way that matters most, as we might just about say of a man with a physically painful condition that he was nevertheless happy, if he resisted despair, self-pity, and so forth, and retained interest and pleasure in other things – and he would have to be at least some of the time moderately *cheerful*. The views of certain philosophers of antiquity, that virtue was sufficient for happiness and that the good man could be happy on the rack, have been rightly thought before, after, and no doubt during their time to involve some paradox. But if happiness is ultimately incompatible with too much, or too total, suffering, there can perhaps be recognizably moral outlooks which reject the notion that happiness is the concern of our arrangements. It is reported that Luther, when someone proposed *Glücklichkeit* (happiness) as the end of human life, violently rejected the idea and said 'leiden, leiden, Kreuz, Kreuz' ('suffering ... the Cross ...'). Here there could be a view that man's sin and distance from God was such that only a life of penitence and consciousness of one's own and everyone's evil could appropriately respond to the situation. Such a view would no doubt deplore institutions, outlooks, ways of life, which tended to eliminate these, the most basic of man's sufferings, and might only contingently or peripherally approve those which lightened less spiritual sufferings.

To this it might be replied that it only shows that Luther placed man's well-being elsewhere, in eventual reconciliation with God, and that sufferings here were only a means to happiness elsewhere. So happiness is still the point, though happiness elsewhere. But this formulation, to the limited extent that I understand

Luther's outlook, seems to me essentially to misrepresent it: still more, perhaps, some other Protestant outlooks. The point is that there is no *means* open to man towards reconciliation with God, no set of human projects conceivably adequate to secure this result – the gap is too great, and there is merely one sign of hope, Jesus Christ, that God's grace will lift up the undeserving. The devout man will obey the will of God, as best he can in his forlorn condition, and must retain his consciousness of that condition, but not *in order to* secure for himself or anyone else salvation, which is at best a wild hope; and if he is rejected he can have no complaint.

I think that this kind of Protestant outlook could be called a moral outlook – certainly it purports to explain man's situation in relation to what conduct is expected of him, and it indeed speaks of what, on its view, is central to man's happiness. But that happiness is seen as so far off and man as so alienated from the source of it, that it would seem a distortion to represent such a morality as aiming at man's happiness: the aim is rather that life should *mirror*, in suffering and obedience, man's deplorable condition. This is surely a very different sort of outlook from the one that deals directly with happiness, and yet it seems perverse not to call it a morality. One might perhaps say that moralities with a transcendental dimension have a greater logical freedom with respect to their content than moralities which have no such dimension: their transcendental picture speaks of men's general condition and role in terms which may make partially intelligible as a moral outlook attitudes which would be utterly opaque if offered in a purely secular framework.

Even in a secular framework, however, it may be possible to find moral outlooks for which equally 'happiness' seems a poor characterization of their central concerns. Thus certain Romantic outlooks which speak in terms of a free response to life; or of 'honesty' to one's impulses, including destructive ones; or of the significance of extreme experiences – may, any of them, be ineptly described by saying that they have a special view of men's *happiness*. It may be that certain of these outlooks say less about the general framework of morality than they do about certain personal *ideals*. These indeed enter into morality in the sense that for those who respond to such an ideal, it provides a model of life to be lived through and to which a special kind of importance is attached, but they are less concerned with what rules, institutions, dispositions, etc., are required in society as a whole. But this raises large issues, since the relation between personal ideals and general social norms is itself an important moral issue.

It would be stupid to try to discuss these last issues in very general terms: the outlooks in question need to be set out and understood in some depth, and that is not something that can be attempted here. But it seems an open question whether some such outlooks may not genuinely cut the link with happiness as the focus of human moral activity. A central question to be asked in considering this will always be, I think, to what extent the moral outlook makes, perhaps tacitly or vestigially, a transcendental appeal of some kind. And even where there is no transcendental appeal in the sense of a reference, such as the religious moralist makes, to something outside human life which provides in some way a pattern for that life; nevertheless, there may be an appeal to something *there* in human life which has to be discovered, trusted, followed, possibly in grave ignorance of the outcome.

As the last phrase indicates, I am not speaking here of such a thing as Marxist morality, which is not our present concern since it is fairly straightforwardly concerned with ultimate happiness: the well-being of men which is envisaged after the destruction of capitalism and the elimination of exploitation will not perhaps merely consist in their being happier, but it will certainly include that. What I rather have in mind is, for instance, something indicated by a phrase of D. H. Lawrence's in his splendid commentary on the complacent moral utterances of Benjamin Franklin: 'Find your deepest impulse, and follow that.' The notion that there *is* something that is one's deepest impulse, that there is a discovery to be made here, rather than a decision; and the notion that one trusts what is so discovered, although unclear where it will lead – these, rather, are the point. The combination – discovery, trust, and risk – are central to this sort of outlook, as of course they are to the state of being in love. It is even tempting to find, among the many historical legacies of Protestantism to Romanticism, a parallel between this combination and the pair so important to Luther: obedience and hope. Both make an essential connection between submission and uncertainty; both, rather than offering happiness, demand authenticity.

Perhaps the outlook I have gestured towards could not possibly constitute a complete morality, because it has nothing, or not enough, to say about society, and hence not enough to say about even one man's life as a whole. Perhaps even so far as it goes it rests on an illusion. But the very fact that it exists and has power demands some response from anyone who thinks it evident that general happiness must be the focus of morality; as does the religious morality, in so far as its outlook (as in our extreme Protestant example) radically differs from a purely secular outlook. For granted that its transcendental claim is false, human beings must have dreamed it, and we need an understanding of why this was the content of their dream. (Humanism – in the contemporary sense of a secularist and anti-religious movement – seems seldom to have faced fully a very immediate consequence of its own views: that this terrible thing, religion, is a *human* creation.) Men do, as a matter of fact, find value in such things as submission, trust, uncertainty, risk, even despair and suffering, and these values can scarcely all be related to a central ideal of *happiness*. And if we find some explanations, psychoanalytical, perhaps, or even in some cases zoological, of such attitudes, and also come to regard them as aberrancies which we seek to reduce, then certainly we are changing the world from the standpoint of a certain morality, not merely making the world more responsive to what morality unquestionably is.

'Well-being' was the point from which we started; we have been concerned recently with taking that as 'happiness'. Perhaps it might be said that even if some sorts of moral ideas reject happiness as the central notion, there is still a wider, yet contentful, notion of well-being in which they do not reject that. It is a real question, and I do not know the answer. On the one hand, the most extreme cases seem to leave us with a notion of well-being which is really at no great distance from 'being as men ought to be'. where no content is

left. On the other hand, in characterizing these outlooks, one speaks of what men in fact find value in, or
need, or want; and if someone said – obscurely enough –
that men *need* a world in which there is risk, uncertainty,
and the possibility of despair, then a morality which
emphasized this, as opposed to moralities which want
as much as possible tidied up, might still be said to be
concerned with men's well-being. Something will still
be excluded by the use of this term: systems of values
or precepts which paid no attention at all to what we
can understand men as needing or wanting.

UTILITARIANISM

IN discussing the question whether any moral outlook must ultimately be concerned with human happiness, I have not supposed that question to be the same as the question whether all moral outlooks must be one or another version of *utilitarianism*. Obviously they are not the same question if we take the narrowest sense of 'utilitarianism', which holds that there is just one moral principle, to seek the greatest happiness of the greatest number; that 'happiness' here means pleasure and the absence of pain; and that the one moral principle – since it is the one moral principle – is to be applied to each individual situation ('act-utilitarianism'). Obviously there are all sorts of ways in which a morality can be ultimately concerned with human happiness without being identical with *that*. But I think also that there are ways in which morality can be ultimately concerned with human happiness without being identical with utilitarianism even taken in a more extended sense.

A difficulty in discussing this issue is a lack of agreement about how extensively the term 'utilitarianism' may properly or sensibly be used. The term has sometimes been used to include moral outlooks which do not have anything specially to do with happiness or pleasure at all; in this sense, it is used to refer to any outlook which holds that the rightness or wrongness of an action always depends on the consequences of the action, on its tendency to lead to intrinsically good or bad states of affairs. This very broad sense – which is probably better represented by the word 'consequentialism' than by 'utilitarianism' – is not my concern here; we are interested only in views of this kind which do take *happiness* as the one intrinsically good thing, at which actions and social arrangements are supposedly aimed. But that restriction still leaves a lot of room for different sorts of utilitarianism.

To discuss in a vacuum what might or might not count as a recognizable form of utilitarianism would be a purely verbal and pointless exercise. The question can only be approached by asking what the *point* of the utilitarian outlook on morality is; and that can be discovered not merely, nor principally, by consulting what Bentham and J. S. Mill and other classical exponents of the system had in mind, but by considering what the attractions of the utilitarian outlook are for moral thought. I think that there are four major ones: this is not to deny that these are, in ways worth exploring, related to one another. First, it is non-transcendental, and makes no appeal outside human life, in particular not to religious considerations. It thus helps, in particular, with the entirely reasonable demand that morality now should be obviously free from Christianity. It can even seem to help – because of a certain conservatism which I shall consider later – with a demand far less reasonable, indeed rightly perceived by Nietzsche to be idiotic, that the morality thus freed from Christianity should be very much the same as the one previously attached to Christianity. In more radical hands, however, utilitarianism promises more radical change.

Second, its basic good, happiness, seems minimally problematical: however much people differ, surely they at least all want to be happy, and aiming at as much happiness as possible must surely, whatever else gives way, be a reasonable aim. Now there is a notorious problem at this point about the transition from a supposedly indisputable aim of seeking one's own happiness, to a more disputable aim of seeking other people's happiness, and the unfortunate Mill has been repeatedly beaten over the head by critics for (it is said) trying to make this transition by deductive argument. I doubt whether that was what he was trying to do, but in any case the problem is of no special force against utilitarianism – there is no reason why it, any more than anyone else, should possess a magic formula for arguing the amoralist out of his amoralism. The point is rather that utilitarianism is a *minimum commitment* morality, in this as in other respects: given merely the minimum requirements for being in the moral world, a willingness to consider other people's wants as well as one's own, utilitarianism can get going on this spot. A much more interesting question is whether the 'indisputable' aim of happiness can in fact be made to serve utilitarian purposes. We have already seen some reason, in the previous section, for doubting whether happiness *must* be seen as the aim of human life at all; but even waiving those questions, it is far from clear that any sense in which it is (more or less) indisputably such an end, is also a sense in which utilitarianism can be made to work on it. This is a central issue: we shall be in a better position to consider it when we have looked at the third and fourth attractions of utilitarianism.

Its third attraction is that moral issues can, in principle, be determined by empirical calculation of consequences. Moral thought becomes empirical, and on questions of public policy, a matter of social science. This has always been found by many one of the most gratifying features of utilitarianism. It is not that the calculations are thought to be easy, or even practically possible in many cases; the charm lies rather in this, that the nature of the difficulty is at least quite un-mysterious. All moral obscurity becomes a matter of technical limitations.

Fourth, utilitarianism provides a common currency of moral thought: the different concerns of different parties, and the different sorts of claims acting on one party, can all be cashed (in principle) in terms of happi-ness. This provision, importantly, has the consequence that a certain kind of conflict, well-known to some other moral outlooks, is impossible – the conflict, that is to say, of two claims which are both valid and ir-reconcilable. Under some other systems, a man may come to be in a situation in which (as it seems to him) whatever he does involves doing something wrong. For utilitarianism, this is impossible. The various claims he may feel on him can be brought to the common mea-sure of the Greatest Happiness Principle, and there can be no coherent idea of a right or wrong thing to do, other than what is, or is not, *the best thing to do on the whole*: and if two courses come out equal, then it really cannot matter which he does. As against this, many people can recognize the thought that a certain course of action is, indeed, the best thing to do on the whole in the circumstances, but that doing it involves doing something wrong. This is a thought which for utilitarianism must, I think, ultimately be incoherent. This is one reason for saying (what is certainly true) that for utilitarianism, tragedy is impossible; but it has wider, if not deeper, consequences than that.

The utilitarian may be able to move back a little towards this type of thought, by invoking such things as the desirable social consequences of people being a bit squeamish about certain actions, even when those are, in the circumstances, the best available: we shall come back to that type of argument later on. But what he is bound to do as a utilitarian is to regard as an indisputable general aim of moral thought, the reduction of conflict, the elimination wherever possible of value conflicts without remainder. Here, as elsewhere, he is concerned with efficiency: the generation of conflicts is a sign of inefficiency in a value system, and utilitarianism has a general device for eliminating or solving them. But some might wonder whether such efficiency was an indisputable aim. One can certainly reduce conflict, and make life simpler, by cutting down the range of claims one is prepared to consider; but in certain cases, that might seem not so much a triumph for rationality, as a cowardly evasion, a refusal to see what is there to be seen (we may ask here, once more, whether defused subjectivism really leaves everything where it was).

So even the attractiveness of utilitarianism's fourth attraction may be importantly disputed. Other difficulties crowd in when one considers what it presupposes. For we are going to be able to use the Greatest Happiness Principle as the common measure of all and everybody's claims, only if the 'happiness' involved is in some sense *comparable* and in some sense *additive*. Only if we can compare the happiness involved for different people and over different outcomes, and also put them together into some kind of General Happiness, can we make the thing work. At a technical level these problems have been the concern of such subjects as welfare economics and preference theory, which have laboured within very artificial assumptions and with only moderate success to deal with them for economic theory. Here we are concerned with more general difficulties. If the 'happiness' involved is to be such as to allow utilitarianism to deliver on its third and fourth promises, can it also be the indisputable aim which was promised in the second?

The answer to that seems to be just 'no'. Bentham offered an account of happiness, namely as pleasure and the absence of pain, which was supposed very clearly to deliver on all the promises at once; but even if it had satisfied (as of course it did not) the conditions of being calculable, comparable, and additive, it failed the condition of being an indisputable objective: the more it looked like the sort of pleasure that could conceivably be dealt with in those quasi-arithmetical terms, the less it looked like something that any rational man must evidently be aiming at – as Mill came, if uneasily, to see. If, on the other hand, the conception of happiness is made generous enough to include anything that might reasonably be aimed at as a satisfying life or ingredient of a life – then it less and less looks like something which could fit in with the third and fourth conditions. Apart from anything else, there is the difficulty that many things which people actually include in the content of a happy life are things which essentially involve other values, such as integrity, for instance, or spontaneity, or freedom, or love, or artistic self-expression; and not only can they not be treated in the way that the third and fourth conditions require of utilitarianism's 'happiness', but there seems, in the case of some of them at least, an actual contradiction in thinking of them as something that could be so treated.

This is the first general difficulty, then, with utilitarianism. Its 'happiness' has to satisfy certain conditions, if the point of utilitarianism is to be retained; and the condition, that it should be indisputably an aim of human aspiration, conflicts with the other conditions which it must satisfy if it is to be treated as utilitarianism requires it to be treated. Faced with this general difficulty, one way in which utilitarianism tends to react is to dispute the values involved in the more intractable conceptions of happiness, as irrational, perhaps, or as hangovers of a past age. Such arguments may involve some interesting points on the way, but their strategy is shamelessly circular: utilitarian rationality is made the test of what counts as happiness, in order to remove that sort of happiness which constitutes an objection to utilitarianism. All that is needed to counter this at the theoretical level is a suitable unwillingness to be bullied.

The problem, however, is not confined to the theoretical level: it occurs drastically at the social level, and an unwillingness to be bullied may here be inadequate, or hard to enforce. In cases of planning, conservation, welfare, and social decisions of all kinds, a set of values which are, at least notionally, quantified in terms of resources, are confronted by values which are not quantifiable in terms of resources: such as the value of preserving an ancient part of a town, or of contriving dignity as well as comfort for patients in a geriatric unit. Again and again defenders of such values are faced with the dilemma, of either refusing to quantify the value in question, in which case it disappears from the sum altogether, or else of trying to attach some quantity to it, in which case they misrepresent what they are about and also usually lose the argument, since the quantified value is not enough to tip the scale. In such matters, it is not that utilitarians are committed to thinking that these other values do not matter; nor are they confined to thinking valuable those things which can presently be handled by cost-benefit analysis. They are perhaps not even bound to think that every social value should eventually be handleable by something like cost-benefit analysis: they might say that they were not committed to the view that the common currency of happiness is money. But they are committed to something which in practice has those implications: that there are no ultimately incommensurable values. Nor is it an accidental feature of the utilitarian outlook that the presumption is in favour of the monetarily quantifiable, and the other values are forced into the apologetic dilemma we have just met. It is not an accident, because (for one thing) utilitarianism is unsurprisingly the value system for a society in which economic values are supreme; and also, at the theoretical level, because quantification in money is the only obvious form of what utilitarianism insists upon, the commensurability of value.

There is great pressure for research into techniques to make larger ranges of social value commensurable. Some of the effort should rather be devoted to learning – or learning again, perhaps – how to think intelligently about conflicts of values which are incommensurable.

These have been difficulties in satisfying utilitarianism's conditions for 'happiness'. The fact that there are these difficulties does not mean, of course, that we can never in any particular case or sort of case arrive at an idea of what the utilitarian solution would be, or of what sorts of things the utilitarian would count. Something would be wrong if this did follow, since clearly we can sometimes do these things: in discussing utilitarianism, we are discussing *something*, and something quite often recognizable. So let us grant that in some cases, at least, we do know what is meant by working out what course of action would lead to the greatest happiness all round. Granted this, we now meet two new difficulties. One is that the process of working out such consequences is itself an activity, which itself in various circumstances possesses various degrees of utility, and this has to go into the sum. The other is that the answer reached by utilitarian calculation of the particular case seems in certain cases to be morally the wrong answer. There exists a kind of utilitarianism, called 'rule-utilitarianism', whose aim is precisely to solve both these difficulties at once, by one and the same device.

The first problem is that any actual utilitarian calculation will take place under conditions of considerable uncertainty and very partial information, so that its results are likely to be unreliable. Moreover, the business of calculation itself takes time; and the disposition to calculate in each case has psychological features which may as a matter of fact impede things which are utilitarianly desirable, such as resolute action. These things being so, it is suggested that better consequences may follow from the practice, not of agents calculating each action, but of their subscribing to certain rules which they apply usually without calculation to particular cases; it is the adoption of these rules which is assessed by appeal to the Greatest Happiness Principle, and not the choice of particular actions.

The same idea is invoked to explain the other fact which otherwise presents a difficulty, that we can easily construct cases – for instance where the conviction of an innocent man is necessary and sufficient to avoid great harms – in which the utilitarian result seems to conflict with what many would regard as the morally right answer: as in this case with justice, so promise-keeping and truth-telling are found to present difficulties under the act-utilitarian interpretation. The rule-utilitarian can, it is hoped, dissolve these difficulties by claiming that all that has to be shown is that the rules or practices of justice, promise-keeping or truth-telling possess positive utility over the alternatives.

This is only a sketch. Many importantly different things can be covered by the term 'rule-utilitarianism', and different things need to be said about them.* All I will try to do here is to suggest one or two points about how far the utilitarian can consistently go in the rule direction; and argue that either he cannot go far enough to solve the second difficulty, or else he has to go so far that he (and everyone else) ceases to be a utilitarian.

It is certainly possible for a utilitarian, without inconsistency, to adopt a general practice for dealing with a certain kind of case, even though some particular applications of the practice produce a result different

*For a detailed and subtle discussion of the issues involved, see David Lyons's important book, *The Forms and Limits of Utilitarianism* (Oxford: Clarendon Press, 1969).

from what would have been reached by individual calculation of those instances. The paradigm of this is the accounting system of many public utilities, who may occasionally send out a bill for some very small sum, even though each bill costs more than that to process: the point being, that it is actually cheaper to send out all bills when due, however small the amount, rather than to interrupt the processes to extract a few bills. Let us call this the 'gas bill model'.

Now the gas bill model deals in actual consequences: the actual consequences of merely applying a rule, on the one hand, and of making a particular interference, on the other. This sort of model, at least, cannot render palatable to a consistent utilitarian a form of argument which invokes neither the actual consequences of a particular choice, nor the actual consequences of the general following of a rule, but the *hypothetical* consequences of an *imagined* following of a rule. Thus the familiar pattern of moral argument, 'how would it be if everyone did that?' cannot have any effect on a consistent utilitarian unless his action really will have the effect of making everyone do it, which is usually pretty implausible. A purely imaginary consequence can no more figure in a utilitarian calculation, than the happiness or unhappiness of purely imaginary persons can. So the gas bill model, at least, cannot in itself get us on the road to that kind of generalization argument.

If the utilitarian wants to justify the use of the generalization argument which deals in imagined consequences, he will have to take a further step away from the actual consequences of particular choices, and deal in terms of the *actual* consequences of people's *thinking in terms of imagined consequences*. But now he seems to be getting further and further away from the original utilitarian advantages. For, first, the supposed calculation of the utility of people's thinking in terms of imagined consequences – as against their working out particular cases; or working out the consequences of more specific rules; or taking the local morality as a going concern; or many other possibilities – this calculation begins to look more and more like bluff. How does he know what the consequences of these various practices might be? Second, he does know one thing, at least: that the more general the provision to which the utilitarian calculation is attached, the more cases there will be in which particular calculation in that case would have produced a different result, so the more tactical disutility he is licensing in his pursuit of strategic utility. In view of the doubtfulness of the strategic utility, this ought to worry him: one of the motivations of utilitarianism, after all, was a hard-headed injunction to think in terms of calculable consequences, and not just to rely on tradition, received practice and so forth.

The more one considers rule-utilitarianism, the more pressing this sort of point becomes. Turning once more to the gas bill model, we can recall that what principally made the uniform practice sensible was the cost of interfering with it. The analogy to this in ordinary moral deliberation is the disutility of calculating particular consequences. But the effect of that argument is cancelled out if we consider a case in which the particular calculation *has already been made*: and this is so in the morally disquieting cases which presented the second kind of difficulty rule-utilitarianism was supposed to deal with. If calculation has already been made, and the consequences of breaking the rule are found better than those of keeping it; then certainly no considerations about the disutility of calculation could upset that result. And, indeed, it is very difficult to see how *anything*, for a consistent utilitarian, could upset that result. Whatever the general utility of having a certain rule, if one has actually reached the point of seeing that the utility of breaking it on a certain occasion is greater than that of following it, then surely it would be pure irrationality not to break it?

This consequence has indeed been drawn by some tough utilitarians, such as J. J. C. Smart. If utilitarianism can be got going at all, then I am sure theirs must be the right attitude to it: it is a special doctrine, not necessarily coincident with contemporary Western moral ideas in all respects, and one must expect it to have what may well seem unpalatable conclusions. Contrary to this, one feature of much modern utilitarian theory is that it is surprisingly conformist. Bentham and Mill regarded the Greatest Happiness Principle as an instrument of criticism, and thought that by appeal to it they could show that many Victorian moral beliefs were mistaken and irrational, as indeed they were. But, except for the well-established areas of sexual and penal reform, themselves inherited from Bentham and Mill, modern utilitarian theorists tend to spend more effort in reconciling utilitarianism with existing moral beliefs than in rejecting those beliefs on the strength of utilitarianism. One recent writer, for instance, has taken great and honest pains to show that public executions could not, as might seem, be justified on utilitarian grounds. He is left with some frank doubts; but these are doubts about the application and formulation of utilitarianism, and not, as they surely should be, doubts about whether public executions might not be reintroduced. This is an absurd case. But more generally all the many human qualities which are valued and yet resist utilitarian treatment, such as an unaccommodating passion for justice; certain sorts of courage; spontaneity; a disposition to resist such things as useful experiments on senile patients or the use of napalm on some people to secure (as it is supposed) the happiness of more people, often elicit from utilitarian theorists attempts to accommodate utilitarianism to those values rather than condemnation of such values as irrational legacies of a pre-utilitarian era. This is no doubt a tribute to the decency and imagination of those utilitarians but not to their consistency or their utilitarianism.

Rule-utilitarianism, as the enterprise of trying to hold on to something distinctively utilitarian, while knocking the rougher edges off it, seems to me a failure. This middle ground is not logically habitable. As opposed to this, one might, on the one hand, take the line of Smart and others, and pursue act-utilitarianism modified only within the recognizable limits of the gas bill model. This is at least consistent with the misguided aims of utilitarianism, and the fact that it yields some distinctive and (to many) unpalatable particular moral results should be a matter of no surprise. If, on the other hand, you desert this territory and start to apply the utilitarian principle to more and more general practices and habits of thought, what you come out with is unlikely to have any distinctively utilitarian content at all.

This capacity of utilitarianism, once detached from the ground level, to annihilate itself, can be illustrated by a brief argument, with which I shall end. Its empirical premises are not, perhaps, beyond doubt. But they are certainly at least as plausible as most of those generally used by utilitarians in such matters.

One disturbing effect of people being active and conscious utilitarians is that it tends to debase the moral currency: a Gresham's Law operates, by which the bad acts of bad men elicit from better men acts which, in better circumstances, would also be bad. There is a simple reason for this: a utilitarian must always be justified in doing the least bad thing which is necessary to prevent the worst thing that would otherwise happen in the circumstances (including, of course, the worst thing that someone else may do) – and what he is thus justified in doing may often be something which, taken in itself, is fairly nasty. The pre-emptive act is built in to utilitarian conceptions, and certain notions of negative responsibility (that you are as responsible for what you fail to prevent, as much as for what you do) are by the same token characteristic of it. This being so, it is empirically probable that an escalation of pre-emptive activity may be expected; and the total consequences of this, *by utilitarian standards themselves*, will be worse than if it had never started.

The utilitarian who is immersed in the system, however, cannot do anything about this; he must think in terms of actual consequences, and nothing in the realm of actual consequences (at least, nothing helpful) will now be effected by some gesture of principle – there is no way in which, from where he is, he can lead a dash to morally higher ground. Stepping back in reflection, however, he can consider how utilitarian aims might have been better realized than they have been in a world of utilitarians interspersed with villains. No doubt they

would have been if there had been no villains – but
that, certainly, is Utopian. What looks more hope-
ful is a state of affairs in which enough people are
resistant to continuing the rot: resistant, for instance,
by there being a range of things that they cannot consider doing, or bring themselves to do, or put up with
being done, whatever other people do or may do. There
is a limit to their pre-emptive activities. Enough people,
enough of the time, it seems, have to be prepared to stick
at doing various things, whatever the consequences may
be. That means that enough people, enough of the time,
do not have to think as utilitarians; they have, quite
definitely, to think as non-utilitarians. Nor will it do for
them to preserve at the back of their mind the utilitarian rationale in coexistence with the required moral
bloody-mindedness. For they have to be able to resist
utilitarian temptation in the most difficult circumstances, when much obvious harm will follow from re-
sisting it, and for that their non-utilitarianism has to
be very deeply engrained.

Some utilitarians have reached, if not quite for these
reasons, something rather like this conclusion, and
have thought that what it showed was that the truth of
utilitarianism could be known to a responsible élite,
but should not be too widely spread among the masses.
Such a proposal is both personally and socially hopeless. Personally, since the state of mind ascribed to the
reflective utilitarian, and the attitude to others it involves could be honestly held, if at all, only by a very
innocent man (as perhaps Sidgwick was), and no reflective man in our age can be that innocent. Socially, because the educational and other institutions required
to embody such a view would have to be quite different

from anything we could now expect or tolerate, or that utilitarianism itself could want.

If all this is true, then the world which the reflective utilitarian must finally settle on as most likely to yield the outcomes he wants, is a world in which the Gresham's Law is defeated because enough people enough of the time are deeply disposed against thinking in a utilitarian fashion. It is not possible that this disposition should coexist with believing in utilitarianism; nor is it acceptable or socially possible that most should have this disposition while others, the utilitarian élite, should believe in utilitarianism. All that is left is that the world which would satisfy the utilitarian's aspirations would be a world from which belief in utilitarianism as an overall moral doctrine was totally absent, except perhaps as a minor and ineffective eccentricity.

So, if utilitarianism is true, and some fairly plausible empirical propositions are also true, then it is better that people should not believe in utilitarianism. If, on the other hand, it is false, then it is certainly better that people should not believe in it. So, either way, it is better that people should not believe in it.